BOMBAY DAAK: DISCOVERING THE KOLIS OF THE SEVEN ISLANDS

DR ANSHUMALI PANDEY

To the Koli community, the eternal custodians of Mumbai's coastal heritage.

This book, "Bombay Daak: Discovering the Kolis of the Seven Islands," is dedicated to the indomitable spirit, rich culture, and enduring legacy of the Koli community. In the heart of a bustling metropolis, your roots run deep, your traditions stand strong, and your presence remains etched in the very essence of Mumbai.

Through the pages of this book, we celebrate your history, your contributions, and your resilience in the face of change. The stories, anecdotes, and insights shared here are a tribute to your unwavering connection to the Arabian Sea, your vital role in shaping Mumbai's identity, and your vision for a sustainable and culturally vibrant future.

May your cultural tapestry continue to enrich the city's diversity, and may your deep-seated love for the sea serve as a beacon of environmental stewardship. This dedication is a token of our appreciation for your role in shaping the Mumbai we know and love today.

With profound respect and gratitude,

Contents

Foreword

(Vaibhav Gawde)

As a son born to a Koli mother, growing up on the shores of Mumbai, I often found myself enchanted by the rhythmic ebb and flow of the Arabian Sea. The waves, like the stories of our people, carried secrets of a history deeply rooted in these seven islands. From my earliest memories, I recall the echoes of fishermen's songs as they cast their nets, their silhouettes etched against the setting sun.

> "*The Seven Islands have been our cradle, a place where, the Kolis, have thrived for generations. Our traditions, folklore, and unwavering connection to the sea have shaped us into a community with a profound bond to this unique land.*"

In this book, you will embark on a journey to discover the heart and soul of the Kolis, a people with a rich heritage that has weathered the tides of time. Through the pages, you will walk the ancient pathways, experience the thrill of the catch, and sense the unity in our tightly-knit community.

This isn't just a book; it's a portal to the essence of Mumbai and the Kolis who've called it home for centuries. As you delve into these stories, you will become a part of the tapestry of our history, hearing the whispers of the sea and the songs of the fishermen that have echoed through generations.

I am honored to introduce you to "Bombay Daak: Discovering the Kolis of the Seven Islands," a book that invites you to witness the world through the eyes of a Maratha-Koli child and to understand the boundless love we hold for our Mumbai and its sea. Enjoy this journey of discovery, and may it leave an indelible mark on your heart, as it has on mine.

Vaibhav Gawde
(Representing the Maratha-Koli Community, Mr. Gawde is an entrepreneur Based out of Mumbai and Goa)

PREFACE

In the bustling heart of modern Mumbai lies a rich history, culture, and tradition, interwoven with the timeless rhythms of the Arabian Sea. This is a story of the Kolis, the indigenous fishing communities whose legacy dates back to the time when this vibrant city was but a collection of seven islands. As the world rushes forward into an era of rapid urbanization, it becomes ever more crucial to look back, to uncover the roots that nourish the ever-growing tree of Mumbai's identity.

Bombay Daak is a journey into the heart of this coastal culture, a cultural odyssey that takes us beyond the gleaming skyscrapers and neon lights to a world where the sea's embrace is both livelihood and lifeline. The Kolis, whose lives are intricately bound to the ebb and flow of the Arabian Sea, offer us a glimpse into the history, traditions, and challenges that have shaped their unique way of life.

As we embark on this journey, we find ourselves exploring the nooks and crannies of Mahikawati, the capital established by King Bhimdev on Mahim Island in the 13th century. We walk the sandy shores where fisherfolk have cast their nets for centuries, feel the rhythm of ancient melodies, and savor the flavors of their culinary heritage. We encounter stories of resilience, community bonds, and a deep-rooted connection to the sea that transcends generations.

Bombay Daak is not just a story; it is an invitation to engage with the Kolis' past, present, and future. It is a bridge between the modernity of Mumbai and the enduring traditions of its coastal natives. It is an acknowledgment of the Kolis' significance in shaping the city's cultural mosaic and the challenges they face in an evolving urban landscape.

Through this book, we hope to celebrate the Kolis' contributions, honor their heritage, and highlight their aspirations for the future. We invite you to journey with us, to discover the Kolis of the Seven Islands, and to gain a deeper appreciation of the rich history and culture that continue to thrive amidst the bustling metropolis of Mumbai.

Welcome to Bombay Daak. Your voyage of discovery begins here.

Dr Anshumali Pandey

PROLOGUE

In the Heart of Seven Islands, a city rises from the mist of time and memory. A city where stories intersect, weaving a tapestry of life, tradition, and transformation. It is a city of many names, but perhaps the most evocative is Bombay. And at its heart lies a tale as old as the Arabian Sea.

Beyond the modern skyline, bustling markets, and the kaleidoscope of cultures, beyond the glitz and glamour, there is a story that transcends centuries, connecting the past to the present. It is a tale of resilience and adaptation, of culture and tradition, of a community whose roots are as deep as the ocean itself—the Koli community.

This book, "Bombay Daak: Discovering the Kolis of the Seven Islands," embarks on a journey through time and tide, unearthing the heritage and tales of the Kolis—the original inhabitants of the Seven Islands that make up modern-day Mumbai. As we navigate through their history, culture, and contemporary contributions, we are invited to explore the dynamic interplay between tradition and modernity, preservation and adaptation, and the sea and the city.

From the reign of King Bhimdev to the thriving metropolis of Mumbai, we uncover the Koli community's significant role in shaping the city's identity. Their story is etched into the shoreline, a living testament to their enduring bond with the Arabian Sea.

The prologue is but a whisper of the tales that await within these pages. So, embark with us on this captivating journey—a voyage into the heart of Seven Islands, where the Koli culture has thrived, and continues to thrive, against the backdrop of a constantly evolving, vibrant city.

PROLOGUE

As we turn the pages of history, culture, and community, we uncover the stories that connect the Kolis of the past to the Kolis of today—a bridge spanning generations, revealing the beauty of Mumbai's oldest storytellers, the Koli community....

I

Bombay Daak

'THE IMPERIAL INDIAN MIAL' (Calcutta Bombay Service) East Indian Railway

In the heart of India, in the late 19th century, when the railways were still in their infancy, a unique and unexpected legend was born. It was a story woven into the very fabric of the subcontinent, a tale of trains, culinary curiosity, and a delightful creature known as the Bombay Mail fish.

The fish was known by its scientific name, Harpadon nehereus, but its journey across India transformed it into something more. As these fishes were transported in the mail trains that ferried letters, parcels, and passengers across the country, they acquired a name: the Bombay Mail fish. Over time, this name was affectionately shortened to "Bombail" or "Bombil."

In those days, the British Empire had set its sights on an ambitious endeavor, one that would forever transform the face of the Indian subcontinent: the expansion of the railway network. The idea was not merely to lay tracks of steel but to weave a web of connectivity that would bind the diverse regions of India together. This network was envisioned as the lifeblood of the empire, enabling efficient transportation and the seamless movement of people and goods across the vast expanse of the subcontinent.

The inception of India's railway system can be traced back to Madras in 1832 when the earliest railway proposals were put forward. The first railway line in India, known as the Red Hill Railroad, was constructed under the supervision of Arthur Cotton with the primary purpose of transporting granite for road-building. This railway extended from the Red Hills in Chennai to the Chintadripet bridge in Madras and was inaugurated on 12th September 1837. Notably, the Red Hill Railroad was exclusively employed for the transportation of freight.

In 1845, Arthur Cotton embarked on the construction of the Godavari Dam Construction Railway at Dowleswaram in Rajahmundry. This railway was established to facilitate the supply of stone required for the construction of a dam over the Godavari River. In a similar vein, Proby Cautley constructed the Solani Aqueduct Railway in Roorkee in 1851. This railway served the purpose of transporting construction materials for an aqueduct spanning the Solani River. It is worth noting that these railways were disassembled upon the completion of their respective projects and no longer exist today.

The debut of passenger rail services in India was realized through the efforts of the Great Indian Peninsula Railway, with the first passenger train commencing its operation on 16th April 1853. This historical journey was hauled by three steam locomotives, named Sahib, Sindh, and Sultan, and accommodated 400 passengers in 14 carriages. The railway track utilized a broad gauge of 1,676 mm (5 ft 6 in) and connected Bori Bunder in Mumbai to Thane.

The development of India's railway infrastructure continued, with the creation of the Thane viaducts, the nation's first railway bridges. These viaducts were constructed to traverse the Thane creek and were a part of the Mumbai-Thane line extension to Kalyan, which occurred in May 1854.

The momentum of railway expansion was not confined to the west, as Eastern India witnessed the inauguration of its first passenger train. This railway route covered a distance of 39 km, running from Howrah, near Kolkata, to Hoogly, and commenced on 15th August 1854.

The southern regions of India also embraced the railway revolution, with the debut of the first passenger train in South India. This inaugural journey spanned 97 km and traveled from Royapuram - Veyasarapady in Madras to Wallajaroad in Arcot, commencing on 1st July 1856.

Now, coming back to our story of Bombay Daak; one of the earliest and most crucial routes to be established was the one connecting Bombay, with Calcutta, the thriving city on the eastern coast. This endeavor was particularly significant, given the vast geographical expanse it aimed to cover. Bombay, the economic and administrative heart of British India, needed a direct and efficient connection to Calcutta, a city of equal prominence and strategic importance.

The construction of this pioneering railway line was a Herculean task, one that called for relentless dedication and perseverance. It entailed laying thousands of miles of tracks across diverse terrains, ranging from the arid plains of the Deccan Plateau to the lush forests of Central India and the winding rivers of Bengal. Engineers, laborers, and surveyors toiled relentlessly, often braving harsh conditions, inhospitable landscapes, and unexpected challenges. These tireless efforts paved the way for a mode of transportation that would eventually become the backbone of the Indian subcontinent.

When the Bombay-Calcutta railway route was finally completed, it marked the culmination of a monumental achievement. It was not just a railway line but a conduit for the exchange of culture, trade, and ideas. This groundbreaking railway connected the bustling port of Bombay, where goods from across the world arrived, with Calcutta, the melting pot of diverse communities and cultures. It became the catalyst for the economic and social transformation of India.

The railway brought with it the promise of swift and efficient movement. It allowed merchants to transport their wares more quickly, reducing the time it took for goods to reach distant markets. People could travel from Bombay to Calcutta in a fraction of the time it would take by traditional means, thereby facilitating tourism, family visits, and cultural exchanges.

The railway was more than just a transport system; it was a lifeline, a thread that stitched together the patchwork of India. It made the vast subcontinent more accessible and integrated, bridging the geographical and cultural divides that had persisted for centuries. The Bombay-Calcutta railway became a symbol of progress, a testament to the power of human ingenuity, and a harbinger of a brighter future for the Indian subcontinent.

This remarkable feat of engineering was the cornerstone of the British Empire's efforts to exert control over India, but it also served as the foundation for an interconnected and interdependent India that would emerge in the decades to come. It was within this web of iron and steam that a humble fish, the Bombay Mail fish, found its path from Bombay to Calcutta, leaving a flavorful legacy that would forever remind us of the enduring power of the railways in shaping history.

The story goes emerged somewhat like this; as the tracks were being laboriously laid and the grand stations took shape along the Bombay-Calcutta railway route, a curious cargo began to traverse this iron lifeline across the subcontinent. This extraordinary commodity was none other than the Bombay Mail fish, a small and unassuming marine treasure whose flavor held the promise of culinary delight that transcended regional boundaries. Its journey from the bustling markets of Bombay to the kitchens of Calcutta was destined to become a captivating tale, one that still tingles the taste buds of connoisseurs and gastronomes in India today.

The bustling markets of Bombay, with their diverse stalls brimming with the bounty of the Arabian Sea, were a rich source of exotic delicacies that would soon captivate the culinary world of Calcutta. Among these treasures was the

Bombay Mail fish, a species known scientifically as Harpadon nehereus. Despite its modest appearance and relatively small size, this fish possessed a unique and flavorful profile that made it the subject of intrigue and culinary curiosity.

As the railway tracks advanced across the country, opening up new frontiers and connecting distant regions, the Bombay Mail fish embarked on its own journey of discovery. It found itself packaged and carefully transported within the confines of the mail trains that would crisscross the subcontinent. This fortuitous association with the postal system earned it the moniker "Bombay Mail fish," a name that would eventually be affectionately shortened to "Bombail" or "Bombil."

The story of how this humble fish made its way from the western coast of India to the eastern shores was an odyssey in itself, marked by the rhythmic clatter of the train wheels and the aromatic wafts of spices that pervaded the mail cars. Packed securely in parcels along with other goods and letters, these fishes ventured across the vast expanse of the country, steadily inching their way eastward.

It was during a brief stopover at one of the railway stations that a curious Bengali traveler, weary from the journey, had his fateful encounter with the enigmatic Bombail fish. As he waited on the platform for the train to continue its journey, his senses were captivated by the tantalizing aroma that wafted from the food vendors. One particular vendor, with a twinkle in his eye, suggested that the traveler try the recently arrived Bombay Mail fish.

Intrigued and in the spirit of adventure, the traveler ordered a serving. What followed was a sensory revelation that left him spellbound. The Bombail, delicately spiced and masterfully fried, transformed into a gastronomic wonder.

Its tender flesh, infused with the flavors of the Indian spices, melted in his mouth, leaving an indelible impression. This chance culinary encounter became a moment of inspiration, and he couldn't resist sharing his newfound discovery with others.

Word of the Bombay Mail fish's culinary charm quickly spread throughout Calcutta. The city's chefs, renowned for their innovation and culinary mastery, welcomed the newcomer with open arms. They realized that the Bombail was not merely a fish but a canvas for their culinary artistry. It could be pan-fried to perfection, added to rich, aromatic curries, or incorporated into delectable seafood dishes.

The bustling streets of Calcutta soon echoed with the joyous chorus of vendors hailing the arrival of fresh Bombail, and homes across the city were filled with the enticing aromas of dishes featuring this newfound delight. The humble fish had transcended its origins and become a culinary legend, emblematic of the interwoven flavors and cultures of India.

With each passing year, the Bombay Mail fish, known as Bombail or Bombay Daak, continued to make its mark on Calcutta's vibrant culinary scene. It transcended regional boundaries and found a place in the hearts and palates of the people of Bengal and beyond. The story of its journey served as a reminder of the incredible connections brought about by the Indian railways, and the enduring legacy of the Bombail fish continues to tickle the taste buds of connoisseurs and enthusiasts, symbolizing the captivating blend of flavors that defines India's rich culinary tapestry.

Word of the Bombay Mail fish's journey from Bombay to Calcutta spread like wildfire, and its name transformed into "Bombay Daak" among the Bengali-speaking population.

Daak, in Bengali, means mail, and the name was a tribute to the trains that brought this culinary treasure to the city.

As the years passed, the Bombay Mail fish not only became a staple in Calcutta's cuisine but also made its way into homes all over India, beloved for its delicate taste and versatility. The story of its journey across the subcontinent served as a reminder of the incredible connections brought about by the Indian railways, tying the diverse regions of the country together in a shared appreciation for the Bombail's unique charm.

Today, the Bombay Mail fish, or Bombail, or Bombay Duck, still graces the plates of many, its rich history and tantalizing flavors keeping the legend alive. It is a testament to the surprising and delightful stories that can emerge from the most unexpected places, a reminder that in the diverse tapestry of India, there is always room for a delicious and humble fish to make its mark on history.

II

Mahikawati: The Kingdom of Silharas

"The 13th-century local King Bhimdev of the Silhara dynasty of the Thane area established his first capital Mahikawati on Mahim island."

In the 13th century, the region now known as Mumbai was not the bustling metropolis we see today but rather a cluster of islands inhabited by local fishing communities. One notable figure from this period was King Bhimdev, who established his capital, Mahikawati, on Mahim Island, leaving a lasting impact on the history of this region.

King Bhimdev's Reign and Legacy:

King Bhimdev, also known as Raja Bhimdev or Bhimdev - I, was a ruler of the Silhara dynasty. His reign is dated to around the late 12th century to the early 13th century AD. He ruled over the islands that make up present-day Mumbai, as well as the surrounding coastal regions.

Bhimdev I was a 13th-century king of the Shilahara dynasty of Thane, Maharashtra, India. He is credited with establishing the town of Mahikawati, which is now the Mumbai suburb of Mahim.

Bhimdev was the son of King Chandradeva. He ascended to the throne in 1260 CE. During his reign, he expanded the Shilahara kingdom and built several temples and forts. He also established Mahikawati as his capital. Mahikawati was located on Mahim island, which is now a part of Mumbai. The island was strategically located on the Arabian Sea coast and was an important trading center. Bhimdev built several temples and forts in Mahikawati, including the Mahim Fort and the Mahakali Temple.

Bhimdev ruled for 35 years and died in 1295 CE. He was succeeded by his son, Krishnadeva. The Shilahara dynasty ruled Thane for over 300 years. They were eventually overthrown by the Yadava dynasty in the 14th century.

The legacy of Bhimdev I is still visible in Mumbai today. The Mahim Fort and the Mahakali Temple are still standing, and they are popular tourist destinations. The name of Mahikawati is also preserved in the name of the Mahim suburb.

Establishment of Mahikawati:

Mahikawati, the capital of King Bhimdev's kingdom, was situated on Mahim Island, one of the several islands that comprise modern-day Mumbai. This island offered strategic advantages, being centrally located and well-connected to neighboring regions. It served as a prominent center for trade, administration, and culture during his rule. Let's elaborate on the significance of Mahikawati, the capital of King Bhimdev's kingdom, and its location on Mahim Island in the context of the 13th century.

Strategic Location of Mahim Island:

Mahim Island, located along the western coast of India, offered King Bhimdev and his kingdom several strategic advantages:

- **Centrally Located**: Mahim Island was situated centrally among the group of islands that later formed modern-day Mumbai. This central position made it an ideal administrative and trade hub. It allowed for efficient governance and facilitated the movement of people and goods across the region.
- **Natural Harbor**: The island's natural features, including its sheltered bay and calm waters, provided a safe natural harbor for ships. This was crucial for maritime

trade, as ships could anchor here and unload cargo without the challenges of rough seas.

- **Trade Routes:** Mahim Island's location along the western coast of India made it well-connected to important trade routes. It was a vital stop for ships traveling along the western coast, making it a prime location for commerce.

Prominent Center for Trade:

During King Bhimdev's rule, Mahikawati on Mahim Island became a bustling center for trade and commerce:

- **Merchant Activities**: The strategic location of Mahim Island attracted merchants and traders from various regions of India and beyond. These traders engaged in the exchange of goods such as spices, textiles, precious metals, and other commodities.
- **Economic Prosperity**: The economic prosperity generated by trade contributed to the growth of Mahikawati. The kingdom benefited from customs duties and trade taxes, further enhancing its economic stability.

Administrative and Cultural Significance:

Apart from trade, Mahikawati served as a hub for administration and culture:

- **Administrative Capital**: Mahikawati was the political and administrative heart of King Bhimdev's kingdom. It housed administrative offices, royal courts, and officials who managed the affairs of the kingdom.
- **Cultural Flourishing**: The Island's central location allowed for the convergence of people from various

backgrounds, leading to a rich cultural exchange. Temples, monuments, and cultural institutions thrived, contributing to the cultural vibrancy of Mahikawati.

Mahikawati on Mahim Island was strategically positioned at the crossroads of trade routes, serving as a pivotal center for trade, administration, and culture during King Bhimdev's rule. Its natural harbor, central location, and economic prosperity made it a significant player in the coastal trade networks of the time, leaving an enduring mark on the historical and cultural legacy of Mumbai.

Contribution to Trade and Commerce:

King Bhimdev recognized the economic potential of the region, which was blessed with abundant natural resources and a favorable location along trade routes. Under his rule, Mahikawati thrived as a trading hub. It facilitated trade not only with other parts of India but also with foreign lands, attracting merchants, traders, and sailors to its shores.

Architectural and Cultural Flourishing:

During Bhimdev's reign, Mahikawati witnessed an architectural and cultural renaissance. Temples, fortifications, and other structures were built, reflecting the rich architectural heritage of the Silhara dynasty. The influence of Hindu culture was prominent, and many temples were dedicated to deities such as Shiva and Vishnu.

Legacy in Modern Mumbai:

While the physical remnants of Mahikawati have largely disappeared due to urbanization, King Bhimdev's legacy endures in the cultural and historical memory of Mumbai. The name "Mumbai" itself is believed to have originated from "Mumbā," the name of the local Hindu goddess Mumbadevi, and "Aai," meaning mother in Marathi. Bhimdev's rule played a crucial role in shaping the early history of the islands that would later become Mumbai.

King Bhimdev's reign in the 13th century left a significant mark on the Mumbai region. His establishment of Mahikawati on Mahim Island facilitated trade, culture, and architecture, contributing to the historical and cultural tapestry of this vibrant city we know today as Mumbai.

The Kolis of the Shilahara kingdom:

During the rule of King Bhimdev in the 13th century, the Koli community played a pivotal role in the coastal region that later became Mumbai. The Kolis were the indigenous inhabitants of these islands and were intimately connected to the sea. Here's a glimpse into the life and contributions of the Koli community during King Bhimdev's rule:

1. Fishing and Maritime Expertise:

The Koli community has a long history of fishing, and during King Bhimdev's reign, they were the primary fishermen of the region. Their expertise in navigating the Arabian Sea and catching various types of fish was invaluable to the local economy. Fish was not only a staple in the diet but also a significant source of income for the community and the kingdom.

2. Economic Contribution:

The Kolis' fishing activities contributed significantly to the kingdom's economy. They provided a constant supply of fresh seafood for local consumption and trade. Their catch was essential for feeding the growing population of the region, including the court and urban centers within the kingdom.

3. Cultural Presence:

The Koli community's cultural presence was an integral part of life in Mahikawati. Their traditional music, dance, and folk arts were a source of entertainment and cultural enrichment. These cultural expressions often found their way into the celebrations and festivals of the kingdom, adding to the diversity and vibrancy of the region.

4. Integral to Trade:

As skilled fishermen, the Kolis played a crucial role in facilitating trade and commerce. The fish they caught were not only consumed locally but also traded with neighboring regions. This trade helped establish Mahikawati as a prominent center for commerce, thanks in part to the Kolis' contribution.

5. Environmental Stewardship:

The Koli community had a deep connection to the sea and the surrounding environment. They were early environmental stewards, understanding the importance of preserving the marine ecosystem for future generations. This commitment to sustainable fishing practices helped maintain the ecological balance of the coastal waters.

6. Resilience in the Face of Challenges:

While King Bhimdev's reign was relatively prosperous, the Kolis faced challenges such as changing weather patterns, natural disasters, and fluctuations in fish populations. However, their resilience, adaptability, and strong sense of community enabled them to weather these challenges and continue their way of life.

During the rule of King Bhimdev, the Koli community in Mahikawati played a vital role in the economic, cultural, and social life of the region. Their expertise in fishing, cultural contributions, and commitment to sustainable practices were essential elements of the kingdom's identity. The legacy of the Koli community during this period is a testament to their enduring presence in the coastal history of Mumbai.

The Koli community continued to play an important role in the development of Mumbai after King Bhimdev's rule. They were instrumental in the construction of the city's first harbor, and they continued to be the primary fishermen and sailors in the region. The Kolis also played a major role in the development of Mumbai's culture and identity.

Today, the Koli community is still an important part of Mumbai. They make up a significant portion of the city's population, and they continue to play a major role in the city's economy and culture. The Kolis are a proud people, and they are rightly proud of their contributions to the development of Mumbai.

III

Mumbai Merger

Merger of the Seven Islands: A British Marvel

To manage the rapidly growing population, the British initiated large-scale land reclamation projects. They connected the seven islands through a series of causeways, creating a single landmass. This ambitious endeavor paved the way for the modern city's expansion.

In the 17th century, as the British East India Company firmly established its presence in Mumbai, they realized the need to address the challenges posed by the rapidly growing population and the limited land available on the original seven islands. To manage these issues and facilitate urban growth, the British initiated large-scale land reclamation projects. These projects were nothing short of remarkable feats of engineering and planning, reshaping the geography of Mumbai and laying the foundation for the modern city we know today.

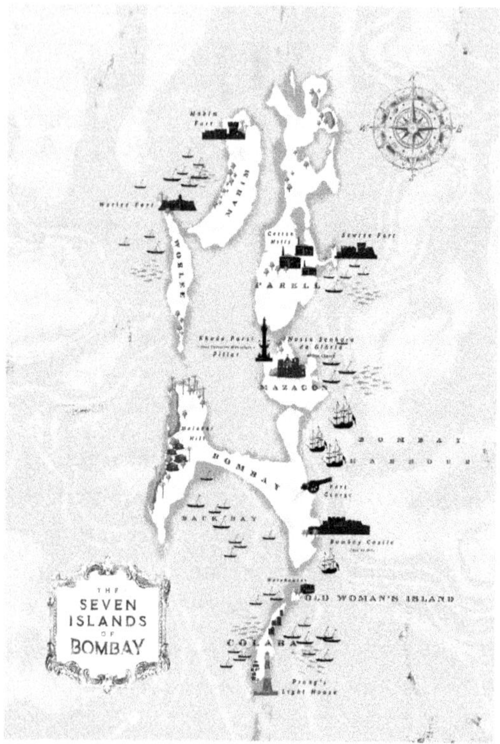

Land Reclamation Begins:

The concept of land reclamation in Mumbai during the British colonial era was a remarkable engineering and urban planning endeavor. It involved the deliberate creation of new land by filling in water bodies, marshes, and shallows, a process that dramatically reshaped the city's landscape. This transformation began with the construction of sea walls and embankments, which were pivotal in safeguarding the shoreline against erosion and the relentless natural forces of the Arabian Sea. The British engineers, influenced by similar projects in Europe, embarked on an ambitious plan to connect the original seven islands of Mumbai into a single contiguous landmass.

- **Creation of New Land**: Land reclamation is a process that involves altering the natural coastline and water features to extend the available land. It often begins with the construction of seawalls, which act as protective barriers against the erosive forces of the sea. Behind these seawalls, various materials such as rocks, rubble, and soil are deposited and compacted to raise the land level, effectively "reclaiming" it from the sea. This created new, usable terrain where there was once water.
- **Protection against Erosion**: Mumbai, being a coastal city on the western coast of India, was vulnerable to coastal erosion, especially during monsoons and cyclonic events. The Arabian Sea posed a constant threat to the city's shores. To address this issue, the construction of sea walls and embankments was vital. These barriers served to break the force of incoming waves and protect the reclaimed land from being washed away.
- **European Inspiration**: The British engineers working on the land reclamation projects drew inspiration from similar endeavors in Europe, particularly in cities like Amsterdam in the Netherlands and Venice in Italy. These European cities were renowned for their successful land reclamation efforts and had become models for urban development. The British saw the potential in applying similar techniques to transform Mumbai's geography.

- **Ambitious Plan for Unity**: The most ambitious aspect of these projects was the plan to connect the seven separate islands of Mumbai. Each island had its unique character and purpose, but they were fragmented and had limited space for expansion. The vision was to unite these islands, both physically and administratively, by constructing a series of causeways, bridges, and land reclamation projects. This unification was driven by the need to manage the city's growing population and cater to its evolving economic and urban needs.

By connecting the islands and creating new land, the British engineers not only overcame the geographical constraints but also set the stage for the modern city of Mumbai. These projects allowed the city to grow, expand its urban footprint, and accommodate the influx of people and industries. The legacy of this ambitious land reclamation effort is evident in the thriving metropolis we know today, demonstrating the significant impact of urban planning and engineering on the development of cities.

Construction of Causeways and Bridges:

One of the most notable aspects of these projects was the construction of causeways and bridges. The British engineers designed a network of causeways to link the individual islands. These causeways acted as vital links, providing both transportation and stability. The most famous among them is the Colaba Causeway, which connected Colaba Island to the main Mumbai Island. This development made it possible for people and goods to move freely between the islands and marked a significant step towards unifying the region.

- **Network of Causeways**: The British engineers envisioned and executed a network of causeways that served as pivotal links connecting the individual islands of Mumbai. These causeways were elevated roadways or embankments constructed over reclaimed land, effectively bridging the gaps between the islands. By creating a network of causeways, the engineers aimed to overcome the geographical separation of the islands and unify them into a single landmass.
- **Vital Links for Transportation**: The causeways were not just physical connections; they were lifelines for the city. They provided essential transportation links between the islands, allowing people and goods to move freely. Before the construction of these causeways, the islands had limited communication, and traveling between them involved the use of boats or ferries, which could be slow and unreliable, particularly during adverse weather conditions. The causeways revolutionized transportation in Mumbai, enabling a more efficient and dependable means of moving both people and cargo.
- **The Colaba Causeway**: Among the network of causeways, the Colaba Causeway stands out as one of the most famous and significant. This causeway connected Colaba Island to the main Mumbai Island. Colaba was already a bustling area with a prominent military presence and rapidly growing urbanization, and the Colaba Causeway became an indispensable link. It not only facilitated the movement of people but also provided access to important government and military installations in the region.
- **Unifying the Region**: The construction of these causeways marked a significant step towards unifying

the seven separate islands into a coherent and integrated urban entity. It allowed for greater interaction and integration among the island communities and eliminated the isolation that had previously characterized Mumbai. This physical unity laid the groundwork for administrative and social integration, as it became easier for people from different islands to interact, trade, and share resources.

The construction of causeways and bridges was a pivotal part of the British land reclamation projects in Mumbai. These engineering feats not only provided essential transportation links but also played a crucial role in unifying the seven islands into a single, cohesive landmass. They remain a testament to the far-reaching impact of urban planning and infrastructure development on the transformation of cities, enabling Mumbai to grow and evolve into the vibrant metropolis we know today.

Creation of Fertile Lands:

The British land reclamation projects in Mumbai went beyond merely connecting the islands; they also included efforts to create fertile lands by systematically filling in marshes and shallows. This aspect of the projects was vital in addressing the city's growing population and burgeoning urban and agricultural needs. The process involved the strategic deposition of materials like rocks, rubble, and soil to transform previously uninhabitable areas into valuable terrain for both agriculture and urban development.

- **Strategic Filling of Marshes and Shallows**: Marshes and shallows are low-lying, often waterlogged areas that are typically unsuitable for most forms of development. They are prone to flooding and are generally unproductive in terms of agriculture. The British engineers recognized the potential of these areas for expansion and development, so they initiated systematic filling processes. They began by constructing protective barriers, such as sea walls and embankments, to prevent tidal waters from inundating these low-lying regions. Once the barriers were in place, they used a combination of rocks, rubble, and soil to raise the land level.

- **Fertile Lands for Agriculture**: One of the primary goals of reclaiming marshes and shallows was to create fertile lands suitable for agriculture. The reclaimed land, often referred to as "reclaimed alluvium," was rich in nutrients and well-suited for farming. Mumbai's rapidly growing population required a consistent and diverse food supply, making these newly created agricultural lands invaluable. As a result, farming activities flourished in the reclaimed areas, helping feed the city's expanding population.

- **Urban Expansion and Settlements**: The availability of reclaimed land not only served agricultural purposes but also played a pivotal role in the city's urban expansion. As Mumbai's population swelled due to immigration and industrialization, there was a pressing need for additional housing and infrastructure. The fertile grounds created through land reclamation were ideal for urban development. This resulted in the construction of residential areas, markets, and industrial zones on the reclaimed land, accommodating the city's ever-increasing population and businesses.

- **Economic Growth and Development**: The newly created land significantly contributed to Mumbai's economic growth. With fertile soil for agriculture and ample space for businesses and industries, the city attracted settlers and entrepreneurs. The thriving economy of Mumbai, particularly its textile industry and trade, received a substantial boost from the availability of reclaimed land. This economic growth, in turn, fueled further urbanization and development.

The British-initiated projects to create fertile lands through systematic filling of marshes and shallows were a critical component of Mumbai's transformation. These efforts not only ensured a stable food supply through agriculture but also provided the necessary land for urban expansion, housing, and economic development. Over time, the reclaimed lands became integral to the city's growth, attracting settlers, fostering economic activities, and contributing to the rapid expansion of Mumbai into the vibrant, diverse metropolis it is today.

Transformation of Waterfronts:
Mumbai's waterfronts were transformed in this process. What were once natural shorelines were now fortified and developed. This not only provided land for housing and infrastructure but also enabled the construction of ports and docks, setting the stage for Mumbai's rise as a maritime and trading hub.

- **Fortification and Development of Waterfronts**: Mumbai's original natural shorelines were often susceptible to erosion and lacked the stability required for urbanization and economic activities. To address this, the British engineers fortified these shorelines using techniques such as constructing sea walls and embankments. These protective barriers shielded the reclaimed land from the erosive forces of the Arabian

Sea, making it suitable for development.

- **Expansion of Land for Housing and Infrastructure**: The transformation of the waterfronts resulted in the creation of substantial amounts of new land. This reclaimed land became highly valuable for urban development, offering space for the construction of housing, commercial areas, and infrastructure. The expanded urban areas not only accommodated the growing population but also provided the necessary space for administrative buildings, markets, and other amenities that a thriving city required.

- **Ports and Docks**: Perhaps one of the most significant outcomes of this transformation was the creation of space for the development of ports and docks. Mumbai's strategic location along the western coast of India made it an ideal candidate for becoming a maritime and trading hub. With the fortified waterfronts, the British were able to construct modern and efficient ports and docks, which played a pivotal role in facilitating trade and commerce, both within India and internationally. These ports became crucial hubs for the movement of goods, connecting Mumbai to global trade routes.

- **Rise as a Maritime and Trading Hub**: The establishment of ports and docks, coupled with the availability of extensive waterfronts, played a pivotal role in shaping Mumbai's identity as a maritime and trading center. The city's location made it a natural gateway for goods entering and exiting India, and the well-developed ports further enhanced its significance. Over time, Mumbai became a hub for various industries, including shipping, manufacturing, and trade, and it attracted merchants and traders from all over the world.

- **Economic and Cultural Impact**: Mumbai's rise as a maritime and trading hub had far-reaching economic and cultural implications. The city's economic prosperity and cosmopolitan nature attracted people from various regions and backgrounds, contributing to its vibrant and diverse cultural landscape. It also played a central role in India's economy, serving as a key center for trade, industry, and finance.

The transformation of Mumbai's waterfronts through land reclamation projects was a fundamental catalyst in shaping the city's destiny. It fortified and developed the shorelines, expanding the available land for housing and infrastructure, and enabled the construction of ports and docks. This laid the foundation for Mumbai's emergence as a maritime and trading hub, a status it continues to hold to this day, driving economic growth and cultural diversity in the region.

Impact on Urbanization:

The impact of these land reclamation projects on urbanization was profound. The availability of more land allowed the city to grow, accommodate its burgeoning population, and attract businesses and industries. As Mumbai expanded, it became increasingly integrated, eventually evolving into a unified and thriving metropolis.

- **Population Growth and Accommodation**: One of the most immediate and noticeable effects of the land reclamation projects was their role in accommodating Mumbai's rapidly burgeoning population. As people from across India and beyond flocked to the city for employment opportunities, the existing land on the seven islands proved insufficient. The creation of new land through reclamation provided the necessary space for housing and infrastructure. Residential areas and neighborhoods sprang up on the reclaimed land, allowing the city to absorb and provide for its increasing population. This was essential in maintaining social cohesion and meeting the housing needs of the diverse populace.

- **Economic Opportunities and Industries**: With the availability of more land, Mumbai was able to attract businesses and industries. The reclaimed areas became prime locations for manufacturing units, commercial spaces, and warehouses. Mumbai's strategic coastal location and efficient ports further enhanced its appeal as an industrial and trading center. Industries like textiles, shipping, and manufacturing found a conducive environment for growth, driving economic prosperity and contributing to the city's vibrant business landscape.

- **Infrastructure and Modernization**: The land reclamation projects necessitated the construction of modern infrastructure, including roads, bridges, utilities, and transportation networks. As these developments progressed, they significantly improved the overall quality of life in the city. Enhanced infrastructure facilitated the movement of people and goods, made daily commutes more efficient, and ensured access to essential services. This modernization not only improved living conditions but also attracted further investment and development.

- **Integration and Unity**: One of the key outcomes of the land reclamation projects was the integration of the once-separate islands into a single, cohesive metropolis. Prior to the projects, the islands operated somewhat independently, with distinct communities and limited interaction. The causeways and bridges connecting the islands eliminated these barriers, creating a sense of unity and facilitating interaction among residents. This cultural integration and blending of diverse communities gave rise to the cosmopolitan nature of Mumbai, where people from different backgrounds and regions coexisted and contributed to the city's rich cultural tapestry.

- **Evolution into a Thriving Metropolis**: Over time, as Mumbai expanded and integrated, it evolved into a thriving metropolis. The city became a microcosm of India, offering a mix of opportunities, cultures, and lifestyles. Mumbai's dynamic landscape, bustling streets, cultural diversity, and economic significance made it a beacon for people seeking a better life and a place for entrepreneurs and businesses to thrive. It emerged as a cultural, economic, and social epicenter, attracting talent, creativity, and innovation from all corners of the country and the world.

The impact of the land reclamation projects on Mumbai's urbanization was transformative. They not only allowed the city to accommodate its growing population and foster economic development but also contributed to the city's integration and evolution into a unified and thriving metropolis. Mumbai's rise as a dynamic, cosmopolitan hub was significantly influenced by these ambitious endeavors that reshaped its landscape and destiny.

The Legacy of Land Reclamation:
The legacy of the British-era land reclamation projects in Mumbai is prominently visible in the modern skyline of

the city. These projects have had a lasting impact, and their effects can be seen in some of the most iconic and bustling areas of Mumbai, such as Nariman Point and Marine Drive. These reclaimed lands, which were once part of the sea, have been transformed into prime business districts. The legacy of the land reclamation projects goes beyond just physical changes; it has played a pivotal role in shaping Mumbai's economic, cultural, and social landscape.

- **Transforming Mumbai's Geography**: The most apparent impact of the land reclamation projects is the transformation of Mumbai's geography. Areas that were originally part of the Arabian Sea have been extended through systematic filling and embankment construction. This expansion was instrumental in accommodating the city's growing population and its economic needs.
- **Prime Business Districts**: Nariman Point and Marine Drive, two of Mumbai's most iconic areas, have been created through these land reclamation projects. These areas are now prime business districts and are home to numerous corporate offices, financial institutions, and commercial establishments. The reclaimed land has been put to excellent use as the city's economic heart, attracting businesses from various sectors and contributing significantly to Mumbai's economic prosperity.
- **Urban Development and Housing**: The legacy of land reclamation also extends to residential development. The reclaimed lands have been developed to accommodate residential areas, which are in high demand due to the city's population growth. These developments have provided housing for the diverse

populace of Mumbai, contributing to its social and cultural diversity.

- **Infrastructure and Modernization**: The need for robust infrastructure to support the reclaimed lands has driven modernization in Mumbai. The city's infrastructure includes an extensive network of roads, bridges, transportation systems, utilities, and public amenities. These improvements have not only made daily life more convenient for residents but have also attracted further investment and development.

- **Economic Growth and Global Significance**: Mumbai has emerged as India's financial and economic hub, with its global significance being closely tied to its role as a trading and financial center. The reclaimed areas, with their efficient ports, have been essential in driving trade and commerce both within India and internationally. The economic growth and prosperity resulting from these projects have elevated Mumbai's status on the global stage.

- **Cultural and Social Diversity**: The cosmopolitan nature of Mumbai, often referred to as "the city of dreams," is a direct result of the legacy of land reclamation. The city's thriving cultural scene, diverse population, and inclusive atmosphere are characteristics that stem from its role as a melting pot of people and ideas. The blending of various cultures and communities has given Mumbai its unique identity.

The legacy of the British-era land reclamation projects in Mumbai is not only seen in the physical landscape of the city but also in its economic, cultural, and social fabric. These projects have left a profound and lasting impact, turning Mumbai into a dynamic, cosmopolitan metropolis with a thriving economy, a rich cultural heritage, and a diverse population. They stand as a testament to human ingenuity and determination in the face of geographical challenges, reshaping the destiny of a city that continues to capture the world's imagination.

The large-scale land reclamation projects initiated by the British in Mumbai were visionary endeavors. By connecting the seven islands through causeways and creating new land, they set the stage for Mumbai's transformation into the vibrant, diverse, and influential city it is today. This ambitious undertaking paved the way for the city's expansion and remains a testament to human ingenuity and determination in the face of geographic challenges.

IV

The Kolis of the Seven Islands

The Koli Community: An Overview

In the bustling metropolis of Mumbai, amid the cacophony of urban life and the glittering skyscrapers that dominate the cityscape, lies a community whose history and culture are deeply intertwined with the very essence of the city. The Koli community, the original inhabitants of Mumbai, has a rich and diverse heritage that dates back centuries. Their story is not just the story of a community but also a narrative of Mumbai's own evolution from a cluster of seven islands to a thriving global megacity.

The roots of the Koli community can be traced back to the times when Mumbai was a collection of seven islands. The word "Koli" is believed to be derived from the Marathi word "kol," which means boat. True to their name, the Kolis were and continue to be skilled fishermen, mastering the art of navigating the Arabian Sea and casting their nets into its depths. It is their intimate connection with the sea that has defined their identity and way of life for generations.

One of the most intriguing aspects of the Koli community's history is the folklore surrounding their settlement in the region. Local legends speak of the Kolis as the original settlers who tamed the islands of Mumbai, having migrated from Gujarat. These tales, passed down through generations, highlight the deep sense of belonging and stewardship the Kolis have for their land.

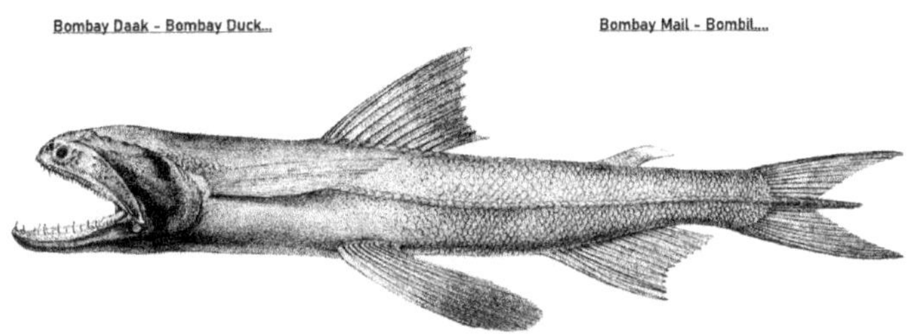

Fishing has been the primary occupation of the Koli community for centuries. Their knowledge of the sea, its tides, and the behavior of fish is not just a skill; it's a heritage. The fishing techniques employed by Kolis have been handed down through generations, each fisherman learning the craft from their fathers and grandfathers. From traditional wooden boats to modern trawlers, the Kolis have adapted their methods to changing times while preserving their rich maritime heritage.

Beyond fishing, the Koli community has a vibrant cultural tapestry woven with rituals, festivals, and customs. Their festivals, such as Narali Purnima and Gudi Padwa, are celebrated with fervor, reflecting their deep connection to both the sea and the land. These festivities are marked by traditional music, dance, and rituals that offer a glimpse into their spiritual and cultural world.

Koli cuisine is a treasure trove of flavors and textures, heavily influenced by their proximity to the sea. The staple of Koli cuisine is, of course, seafood. From bombil (Bombay duck) to pomfret and prawns, the Kolis have a knack for turning the catch of the day into mouthwatering dishes. The famous Koliwada fish fry is a testament to their culinary prowess.

What makes Koli cuisine unique is not just the deliciousness of the food but also the stories behind it. Each dish carries with it a history, a connection to the sea, and a sense of community. Koli cuisine is more than just sustenance; it's a celebration of their identity.

The Koli community, with their deep-rooted history, maritime skills, cultural traditions, and sumptuous cuisine, is an integral part of Mumbai's tapestry. Their story is a testament to resilience and adaptability, as they've weathered the tides of time while holding on to their identity. While the city of Mumbai has grown and transformed, the Kolis remain a living link to its origins, reminding us of the rich heritage that underpins this vibrant metropolis. To truly understand Mumbai, one must delve into the world of the Koli community, for they are the keepers of its past and an enduring presence in its present.

Significance of the Koli Community in Mumbai's History:

Mumbai, the bustling metropolis that stands today, owes much of its identity and character to the Koli community, a vibrant and resilient group of people who have been an integral part of the city's history for centuries. The significance of the Koli community in Mumbai's history is profound, as they played a pivotal role in the city's development, culture, and unique identity. This essay delves into the historical importance of the Koli community and how their legacy continues to shape the city of Mumbai.

The Koli community, also known as Kolis or Kolis of Mumbai, are the indigenous inhabitants of the seven islands that eventually merged to form Mumbai. Their history in the region dates back over 2,000 years, making them one of the oldest communities in Mumbai. Originally, the Kolis were seafarers and fishermen, and their lives were deeply intertwined with the Arabian Sea.

One of the most significant contributions of the Koli community to Mumbai's history is their role as the earliest settlers of the seven islands. These islands—Mazagaon, Parel, Worli, Mahim, Bandra, Colaba, and the Isle of Bombay—formed the foundation upon which modern Mumbai stands. The Kolis were the first to recognize the strategic importance of these islands, given their proximity to the sea and abundant marine resources. They settled here and developed a thriving fishing and trading community.

The Kolis are renowned for their deep knowledge of the sea and fishing techniques. Their expertise in navigating the Arabian Sea and their sustainable fishing practices were crucial to the region's economy. They not only provided sustenance to the local population but also played a pivotal role in facilitating trade and commerce with other coastal regions.

The Koli community's influence extends beyond their economic contributions. They have enriched Mumbai's cultural tapestry with their unique traditions, festivals, and folklore. Festivals like Narali Purnima, celebrating the beginning of the fishing season, and the Koli dance, an integral part of their cultural heritage, have become part of Mumbai's vibrant cultural mosaic.

Throughout Mumbai's tumultuous history, the Kolis have displayed remarkable resilience. As the city evolved from a cluster of islands to a bustling metropolis, they adapted to changing circumstances. While they continue to engage in fishing, many Kolis have diversified their livelihoods to include professions like trade, transportation, and education. This adaptability has allowed them to thrive in an ever-changing urban landscape.

In recent years, there has been a growing recognition of the importance of preserving Koli heritage. Organizations, scholars, and community leaders have undertaken initiatives to document their history, oral traditions, and cultural practices. Museums, cultural centers, and festivals celebrate the rich heritage of the Koli community, ensuring that their legacy endures for generations to come.

The Koli community is not just an integral part of Mumbai's history; they are the very roots from which the city grew. Their contributions in settling the seven islands, sustaining the region through fishing and maritime expertise, and enriching Mumbai's cultural heritage are immeasurable. Their resilience in the face of urbanization and their commitment to preserving their traditions showcase their enduring significance in Mumbai's past and present. To truly understand Mumbai's history and identity, one must recognize and celebrate the invaluable role played by the Koli community.

Mumbai's Early Geographical Landscape:

The story of Mumbai's early geographical landscape is a tale of transformation and evolution that laid the foundation for the vibrant metropolis we know today. This coastal city's history is intrinsically linked to its unique geography and the seven islands that would ultimately merge to create modern-day Mumbai. To understand the significance of these islands and their role in shaping Mumbai's destiny, we must journey back in time to the city's humble beginnings.

Centuries ago, before the skyscrapers and bustling streets, Mumbai was a collection of seven distinct islands—Mazagaon, Parel, Worli, Mahim, Bombay, Colaba, and the Old Woman's island. Each of these islands had its own distinct character, but they were bound together by geography, their shared location along the Arabian Sea.

These islands were not just arbitrary landmasses but strategically located pieces of land in the Arabian Sea. They served as natural harbors and were rich in marine resources, making them ideal for human settlement. The proximity to the sea provided a source of livelihood for the indigenous Koli fishing community, who were among the first settlers of these islands.

The Kolis, known for their seafaring skills, recognized the immense potential of these islands. They became the early inhabitants, establishing fishing villages along the coastlines. These communities thrived on the abundant marine life, and their presence marked the beginning of human habitation in the region.

The geography of Mumbai was not static; it was subject to dynamic natural processes. Over centuries, the islands gradually merged due to land reclamation, geological shifts, and human intervention. The most notable transformation came with the joining of the seven islands into a single landmass, the Isle of Bombay. The British colonial administration played a significant role in shaping Mumbai's landscape through extensive land reclamation projects.

The British, recognizing the strategic and economic importance of Mumbai's natural harbor, initiated massive land reclamation projects in the 18th and 19th centuries. They connected the islands through causeways and filled in the gaps between them with reclaimed land. This expanded Mumbai's territory and set the stage for its rapid urbanization.

As Mumbai expanded geographically, it also underwent significant cultural, economic, and social transformations. The city became a hub for trade, commerce, and industry. Immigrants from across India and beyond flocked to Mumbai in search of opportunities, contributing to its multicultural fabric.

Mumbai's early geographical landscape, with its seven islands, reflects the city's complex history and diverse heritage. The merging of these islands, driven by both natural processes and human intervention, set the stage for Mumbai's evolution into a thriving megacity. Today, as we navigate its bustling streets and towering skyscrapers, it's essential to remember the humble origins of this remarkable metropolis, rooted in the geographical landscape of the seven islands of Bombay.

Role of the Koli Community in Settling and Developing the Seven Islands:

The story of Mumbai's transformation from a cluster of seven islands into the bustling metropolis we know today is incomplete without acknowledging the crucial role played by the indigenous Koli community. Long before Mumbai became a global financial center, the Kolis were the first settlers who recognized the potential of these islands and laid the foundation for the city's development. This narrative explores the remarkable journey of the Koli community in settling and developing the seven islands of Mumbai.

The Kolis are an ancient fishing community with a rich maritime heritage. For centuries, they have been renowned for their seafaring skills and deep understanding of the Arabian Sea. The islands that would later form Mumbai provided an ideal environment for their way of life. The bountiful waters surrounding the islands offered an abundance of fish, making them an attractive destination for fishing communities.

The Koli community was the first to establish settlements on these islands. Their villages dotted the coastlines of Mazagaon, Parel, Worli, Mahim, Colaba, Bonbay, and the Old Woman's Island. These settlements were characterized by their proximity to the sea, a necessity for a community whose livelihood was intricately tied to fishing and maritime trade.

The Kolis' expertise in navigating the treacherous waters of the Arabian Sea was legendary. They developed unique fishing techniques and constructed specialized boats for deep-sea fishing. Their traditional knowledge of tides, weather patterns, and marine ecosystems allowed them to sustainably harvest the sea's resources, ensuring the availability of fish for both their communities and external markets.

As the Kolis prospered, their settlements became important hubs for trade and commerce. They not only met the dietary needs of the local population but also contributed significantly to the regional economy by supplying fish to neighboring areas. Their role as intermediaries between the sea and the mainland enhanced their importance in the evolving society.

The Kolis enriched Mumbai's cultural mosaic with their unique customs, festivals, and folklore. Festivals like Narali Purnima, celebrated with offerings to the sea, and the Koli dance, a reflection of their joyous spirit, became integral to the cultural fabric of the islands.

As Mumbai evolved over the centuries, the Kolis adapted to changing circumstances. Urbanization, land reclamation, and modernization altered the city's landscape, impacting their traditional way of life. Many Kolis diversified their livelihoods, engaging in professions beyond fishing, such as transportation and trade, while others sought education to meet the demands of a rapidly changing city.

Today, efforts are underway to preserve the cultural heritage of the Koli community. Museums, cultural centers, and oral history projects are helping to document their history, traditions, and contributions to Mumbai. These initiatives ensure that the legacy of the Kolis continues to be celebrated and cherished by future generations.

The Koli community's role in settling and developing the seven islands of Mumbai is a testament to their resilience, resourcefulness, and deep connection to the sea. Their early presence and contributions as seafarers, fishermen, and pioneers not only shaped the city's geography but also left an indelible mark on its culture and identity. Today, as Mumbai stands as a symbol of progress and diversity, it's crucial to remember and honor the enduring legacy of the Kolis, the true pioneers of this remarkable metropolis.

Koli Folklore and Legends about Mumbai's Origins:

Mumbai, a city of towering skyscrapers and bustling streets, has a rich tapestry of folklore and legends that often go unnoticed in its modernity. The indigenous Koli community, the earliest settlers of Mumbai, have woven captivating tales that provide intriguing insights into the city's origins. These stories, passed down through generations, offer a unique perspective on Mumbai's mystical beginnings. This narrative delves into Koli folklore and the legends that shroud the birth of Mumbai.

The Tale of Mumbarka

One of the most enduring legends is the story of Mumbarka, the city's namesake. According to Koli folklore, Mumbai was named after a local Koli girl named Mumbarka, who is said to have lived in the region centuries ago. Legend has it that she was a beautiful and kind-hearted maiden. Her name, "Mumbai," is believed to be derived from "Mumbā," which means "mother" in the Koli language, and "Aai," which means "mother" in Marathi. Mumbarka was considered a motherly figure, caring for the fishermen and villagers of the islands.

The Benevolent Spirit of Mumbarka

Mumbarka's legend goes further to depict her as a guardian spirit of the islands. According to folklore, she would often appear in the dreams of the Koli fishermen, guiding them to rich fishing grounds and warning them of impending storms. The Kolis believed that Mumbarka watched over them and ensured their safety at sea.

The Seven Sisters: Islands of Creation

Koli folklore also attributes a mystical origin to the seven islands that would later merge to form Mumbai. According to one legend, these islands were not separate entities but seven sisters, born of the cosmic ocean. Each island had its unique character, and the Kolis revered them as sacred entities. The merging of these islands was seen as a cosmic union, symbolizing the birth of a new world.

The Great Flood and the Magic Kingfisher

Another intriguing legend is the story of a colossal flood that threatened to engulf the islands. In this tale, a magical kingfisher came to the rescue. The bird was believed to have the power to control the seas. It flew across the sky, flapping its wings and causing the waters to recede, saving the islands from destruction. The Kolis saw the kingfisher as a symbol of hope and protection.

Preserving Mumbai's Mythical Heritage

Today, as Mumbai continues to evolve into a modern metropolis, these enchanting legends and folklore persist as a reminder of the city's mystical origins. Efforts are underway to preserve and celebrate this rich heritage through cultural events, storytelling sessions, and educational programs. Museums and cultural centers are dedicated to showcasing Mumbai's diverse history, including its indigenous Koli heritage.

The Koli folklore and legends about Mumbai's origins add a layer of enchantment and mystique to the city's history. While Mumbai has transformed into a bustling urban center, it is essential to recognize and honor the stories that connect its residents to their roots. These legends, steeped in the culture of the Koli community, remind us that Mumbai's history is not only about concrete and steel but also about the magical tales that whisper of its mystical beginnings.

Guardians of the Sea

The Koli community, indigenous to the coastal regions of Mumbai, has a deep-rooted and enduring connection to the sea. For centuries, their traditional occupation of fishing has not only been a means of livelihood but also a way of life that has shaped their culture, traditions, and identity. This narrative explores the profound significance of fishing as the traditional occupation of the Koli community and its integral role in their history and heritage.

The Kolis are renowned for their seafaring skills and their deep understanding of the Arabian Sea. Fishing has been a way of life for generations, with knowledge and techniques passed down from father to son. The art of fishing is woven into the fabric of Koli culture, and it is through fishing that they maintain a profound connection with the sea.

Koli fishermen employ a variety of traditional fishing techniques, adapted over centuries to the unique conditions of the Arabian Sea. Hand-casting nets, traditional boats known as "kattas," and baited hooks are just some of the tools of their trade. The fishing calendar is closely linked to the monsoons and the movement of fish populations, with Kolis relying on their intricate knowledge of tides and currents.

Fishing is not merely an occupation for the Kolis; it is a way of life. Each day, before the break of dawn, Koli fishermen set sail in their boats, seeking the day's catch. The sea is both their workplace and their source of sustenance. The act of fishing is deeply ritualistic, with prayers and rituals performed to ensure a bountiful catch and safe return.

Fishing has not only sustained individual families but also the entire Koli community. The catch is shared among the community members, ensuring that everyone benefits from the fruits of the sea. This communal approach to fishing reflects the tight-knit bonds within the Koli community.

The Koli community's culinary traditions are a testament to their fishing heritage. Their cuisine is centered around seafood, with a rich array of dishes featuring fish, prawns, crabs, and other marine delights. The recipes have been honed over generations, and many are closely guarded family secrets. Koli cuisine has made a significant impact on Mumbai's food culture, with dishes like "Bombil fry" and "Koliwada prawns" becoming local favorites.

While fishing remains central to Koli identity, it has faced challenges in the modern era. Overfishing, pollution, and changing sea conditions have posed threats to the traditional way of life. However, the Koli community has demonstrated remarkable resilience, adapting to new challenges and exploring alternative livelihoods while continuing to preserve their fishing heritage.

Fishing is not merely an occupation for the Koli community; it is the heartbeat of their culture and identity. Through centuries of skillful navigation of the Arabian Sea, they have sustained their families and preserved their traditions. The Koli community's reverence for the sea and their deep connection to it remind us of the importance of preserving traditional occupations that are integral to the cultural fabric of a community and contribute to the rich tapestry of Mumbai's heritage.

Fishing Techniques and Tools Passed Down Through Generations:

The Koli community's mastery of the art of fishing is not merely a skill acquired but a tradition passed down through generations. Their knowledge of fishing techniques and the tools of their trade have been honed over centuries, adapting to the unique challenges posed by the Arabian Sea. This narrative explores the rich legacy of fishing techniques and tools within the Koli community and how they have preserved and evolved this ancient craft.

Casting Nets: The Heart of Fishing

Casting nets is a fundamental fishing technique among the Kolis, one that has been passed down through the ages. These nets, woven meticulously by hand, are cast into the sea to ensnare fish. The process requires precision, timing, and an intimate knowledge of the sea's currents and tides. Younger generations learn this art from their elders, who, in turn, learned it from their ancestors.

The Katta: Traditional Fishing Boats

The Katta, a traditional fishing boat used by the Kolis, is an iconic symbol of their fishing heritage. These sturdy wooden boats are crafted by skilled boatmakers within the community. They are designed to withstand the challenging conditions of the Arabian Sea. The knowledge of Katta construction and repair has been preserved and passed on through generations, ensuring the continued use of these boats.

Baited Hooks and Hand Lines

In addition to net casting, Kolis also employ baited hooks and hand lines for fishing. These hooks are often made from locally sourced materials and are carefully baited to attract various types of fish. The art of crafting effective hooks and using them skillfully is taught within families and communities.

Navigating the Tides and Seasons

Fishing is not a one-size-fits-all endeavor for the Kolis. Their techniques vary with the seasons and the movements of fish populations. Different fish species are more abundant at certain times of the year, and Kolis adjust their fishing techniques accordingly. This intricate knowledge is handed down from elders who have spent a lifetime on the sea.

Rituals and Superstitions

Fishing among the Kolis is not just a matter of practical skill; it is imbued with rituals and superstitions. Before setting out to sea, fishermen often perform religious ceremonies and rituals to ensure a safe and bountiful catch. These practices, steeped in tradition, are shared from one generation to the next.

Challenges and Innovation

While traditional techniques are paramount, the Kolis have also embraced innovation. They have incorporated modern tools and technologies, such as GPS and sonar equipment, to enhance their fishing expeditions. This adaptability reflects the community's commitment to preserving their way of life while meeting the challenges of the modern world.

The fishing techniques and tools of the Koli community are not just practical skills; they are a cultural legacy passed down through generations. They represent an intimate connection to the sea and a commitment to sustaining their families and communities. As the Kolis continue to navigate the shifting tides of tradition and modernity, their enduring knowledge of fishing techniques and tools remains an integral part of their identity and heritage.

Tales of Courage and Resilience on the Arabian Sea:

The Arabian Sea, with its unpredictable tempests and treacherous waves, has long been both a source of livelihood and a formidable adversary for the Koli community. The tales of courage and resilience on the Arabian Sea are a testament to the indomitable spirit of Koli fishermen who, for generations, have ventured into its depths to provide sustenance for their families and communities. This narrative pays tribute to the brave souls who have confronted the challenges of the sea and emerged stronger through their courage and resilience.

The Arabian Sea, while teeming with marine life, is known for its capricious nature. Violent storms, towering waves, and sudden squalls have claimed countless lives and vessels over the centuries. Yet, the Koli fishermen have forged a unique bond with the sea, venturing out daily, driven by their determination to bring home a bountiful catch.

Stories abound of Kolis who have encountered ferocious storms at sea. These tempests, with their deafening roars and towering waves, test the mettle of even the most seasoned fishermen. The courage displayed by Kolis in navigating through these tempests, often risking their lives to secure their catch, is the stuff of legend.

In times of peril, the camaraderie among Koli fishermen shines brightest. Tales are told of daring rescues at sea when one boat comes to the aid of another in distress. These acts of selflessness, borne out of the understanding that their lives are intertwined on the sea, exemplify the strong bonds within the Koli community.

Some stories stand out as legendary feats of survival. There are accounts of fishermen who, lost at sea for days, survived by sheer determination and resourcefulness. These tales of resilience, often handed down through generations, inspire younger Kolis to persevere in the face of adversity.

The stories of courage and resilience on the Arabian Sea are more than just narratives; they are a source of inspiration for the entire Koli community. They embody the spirit of the Kolis, who view the sea not only as a means of sustenance but as a force that tests their resolve and forges their character.

The oral tradition of sharing these stories ensures that the lessons of courage and resilience are passed from one generation of fishermen to the next. Young Kolis grow up listening to the tales of their forefathers, instilling in them a deep respect for the sea and an unwavering commitment to their traditional occupation.

The tales of courage and resilience on the Arabian Sea are a testament to the fortitude of the Koli community. These stories remind us that, despite the hardships and dangers they face, Koli fishermen continue to brave the tempests of the Arabian Sea, driven by their unwavering commitment to their families and their enduring connection to the sea. Their courage and resilience are a source of inspiration, not only for their own community but for all who hear their tales of triumph over the formidable forces of nature.

Navigating Life's Tides: Koli Family and Society

The Koli community, indigenous to the coastal regions of Mumbai, possesses a rich tapestry of family structures and traditions that have been integral to their way of life for generations. These structures, deeply rooted in their culture and history, play a vital role in shaping the social fabric of the Koli community. This narrative delves into the family structures and traditions that bind Koli families together and define their unique identity.

The Koli family is typically extended, comprising multiple generations living together or in close proximity. The concept of joint families fosters a sense of unity and support. Elders are revered and play a central role in decision-making, offering wisdom and guidance to younger generations.

Within the Koli community, the family unit extends beyond blood relations. Neighbors, friends, and even fellow fishermen often become an integral part of the extended family. This sense of community is crucial in a profession where cooperation and mutual support are essential for survival.

Family members often have specific roles and responsibilities within the household. While men predominantly engage in fishing, women are responsible for managing the home, preserving cultural traditions, and sometimes assisting in the fishing activities. This division of labor reflects the Koli community's traditional values.

Marriage is a significant milestone in Koli family life, marked by elaborate customs and ceremonies. Arranged marriages are common, with families playing a crucial role in selecting suitable partners. The wedding rituals, including traditional songs and dances, are a vibrant celebration of Koli culture.

Elders in the Koli family are highly respected and serve as the custodians of traditions and wisdom. They are instrumental in passing down knowledge of fishing techniques, family history, and cultural practices to younger generations. Their guidance is considered invaluable.

Oral traditions are a vital part of Koli family life. Elders often share stories of their ancestors, the sea, and the community's history. These stories are not only a means of preserving cultural heritage but also a source of entertainment and education for younger family members.

Koli families take great pride in celebrating cultural and religious festivals. Festivals like Narali Purnima (coconut festival) and Gudi Padwa (Marathi New Year) are observed with enthusiasm, often involving the entire family in elaborate rituals and feasting.

The family structures and traditions within the Koli community play a pivotal role in preserving their cultural identity and heritage. They serve as a link between generations, ensuring that the values, customs, and knowledge of the Koli way of life are passed down intact.

Koli family structures and traditions are not merely a reflection of their culture; they are the very foundation upon which the community's resilience and identity are built. In an ever-changing world, these structures provide stability, unity, and a profound sense of belonging. They are a testament to the enduring strength of the Koli community and the importance of family in sustaining their way of life.

Marriage Customs and Ceremonies:

Marriage is a sacred institution in the Koli community, deeply rooted in tradition and cultural significance. Koli marriage customs and ceremonies are a vibrant celebration of love, family, and community, reflecting the rich heritage of this indigenous coastal group in Mumbai. This narrative explores the elaborate rituals and ceremonies that make Koli weddings a unique and cherished part of their culture.

Arranged Marriages: The Foundation

In the Koli community, arranged marriages are the norm. Families play a pivotal role in the matchmaking process, considering factors such as social compatibility, family background, and shared values. Elders are typically consulted, and their wisdom guides the selection of suitable partners.

The Engagement Ceremony: Formalizing the Bond

The engagement ceremony, known as "sakharpuda" or "agran," marks the formalization of the engagement between the couple. This event is a joyful occasion, bringing together family and friends to exchange gifts and blessings.

The groom's family typically presents the bride with a sari, sugar, and jewelry as symbols of their commitment.

Haldi Ceremony: A Ritual of Purity

The haldi ceremony is a pre-wedding ritual where a paste made from turmeric, oil, and water is applied to the bride and groom's bodies. It is believed to purify and beautify the couple before their wedding day. The haldi ceremony is a festive occasion filled with song and dance.

Mehendi Ceremony: Intricate Artistry

The mehendi ceremony involves the application of henna designs to the bride's hands and feet. This intricate artistry is not only a form of adornment but also a symbol of love and good fortune. The mehendi ceremony often includes music and dancing.

The Wedding Day: A Grand Affair

Koli weddings are grand affairs, often held in specially decorated venues. The ceremony begins with the "varat," where the groom, accompanied by a procession of family and friends, arrives at the bride's home. This is a joyous moment, marked by music and dancing.

The Wedding Rituals

The wedding rituals themselves are steeped in tradition. The bride and groom exchange vows in the presence of a priest, with the sacred fire as a witness. The exchange of garlands, known as "varmala," symbolizes their acceptance of each other.

Blessings and Feasting

Following the wedding ceremony, blessings are offered to the newlyweds by family members and elders. The celebrations continue with a lavish feast, featuring traditional Koli dishes and other delicacies.

Post-Wedding Rituals

After the wedding, the bride is welcomed into the groom's family with rituals such as "gruhapravesh," where she enters her new home for the first time. The couple's life together begins with the blessings of their families and community.

Preservation of Tradition

Koli marriage customs and ceremonies are not only a celebration of love but also a preservation of cultural heritage. They showcase the deep sense of community and family that are central to Koli identity. While modern influences have introduced some variations, the core traditions of Koli weddings remain a testament to their enduring culture.

Koli marriage customs and ceremonies are a vibrant reflection of the community's rich culture and traditions. These rituals celebrate the union of two individuals, the coming together of families, and the continuity of Koli heritage. They are a testament to the enduring values and sense of community that define the Koli way of life in Mumbai's coastal regions.

Stories of Love and Relationships within the Community:

Within the vibrant tapestry of the Koli community's cultural heritage are stories of love and relationships that have transcended time and tradition. These tales of devotion, unity, and resilience exemplify the deep bonds that form the foundation of Koli families and communities. This narrative explores some of these heartwarming stories that have been cherished for generations.

The Love that Defied Caste Barriers

In the not-so-distant past, the Koli community faced caste-based discrimination and social barriers. Yet, love knows no boundaries. One enduring story tells of a Koli fisherman who fell in love with a woman from a higher caste. Despite societal pressure and prejudice, their love prevailed. Their story became a symbol of love's power to transcend prejudice, eventually leading to greater acceptance and unity within the community.

The Tale of a Seafarer's Longing

The sea is both a provider and a separator in the lives of Koli fishermen. Many stories revolve around the longing and resilience of couples separated by the perils of the sea. These tales recount the unwavering love of wives who anxiously await their husbands' return, praying for their safe homecoming. The reunion of these couples, often celebrated with community gatherings, is a testament to the endurance of love in the face of adversity.

A Mother's Sacrifice for Her Son's Love

In one poignant story, a mother's love knows no bounds as she sacrifices her own wishes to ensure her son's happiness. Faced with societal expectations and opposition, she ultimately supports her son's choice of a life partner. Her selflessness and acceptance become an example of the unconditional love that binds Koli families together.

Community Celebrations of Love

Love stories within the Koli community are often celebrated collectively. Community members come together to rejoice in the union of two souls, with music, dance, and feasting. These celebrations reflect the communal spirit and the importance of shared experiences within the Koli community.

Love Amidst the Trials of the Sea

Koli fishermen often find love and companionship in their fellow fishermen. These couples navigate the challenges of the sea together, relying on each other for support and strength. Their love stories exemplify the resilience and unity that define the Koli way of life.

The Legacy of Love

These stories of love and relationships within the Koli community are not merely anecdotes but a testament to the enduring values of unity, resilience, and acceptance. They underscore the significance of love in overcoming obstacles and strengthening the bonds that hold families and communities together.

The stories of love and relationships within the Koli community are a celebration of human emotion, unity, and the enduring spirit of a community rooted in tradition. They remind us that love transcends societal barriers, provides strength in times of adversity, and forms the very heart of the Koli way of life in Mumbai's coastal regions.

Celebrating Diversity: Religious and Cultural Festivals in the Koli Calendar

The Koli community, deeply rooted in Mumbai's coastal regions, celebrates a diverse tapestry of religious and cultural festivals that reflect their rich heritage and traditions. These celebrations are not only occasions for rejoicing but also opportunities for strengthening communal bonds and preserving the unique identity of the Koli community. This narrative explores some of the most significant festivals in the Koli calendar.

Narali Purnima: The Coconut Festival

Narali Purnima, also known as the Coconut Festival, is one of the most eagerly awaited festivals among the Kolis. Celebrated on the full moon day in the month of Shravan (usually in August), it marks the beginning of the fishing season after the monsoon. The highlight of the festival is the offering of coconuts to the sea as a symbol of gratitude and a prayer for a safe and bountiful catch. This unique tradition reflects the Kolis' deep reverence for the sea, which sustains their livelihood.

Ganesh Chaturthi: The Arrival of Lord Ganesha

Ganesh Chaturthi is a widely celebrated Hindu festival in Mumbai, and the Koli community enthusiastically participates in the festivities. Kolis often set up elaborately decorated idols of Lord Ganesha in their homes and communities. The immersion of these idols in the sea, accompanied by processions and cultural performances, is a spectacular sight and a testament to the religious and cultural diversity of Mumbai.

Diwali: The Festival of Lights

Diwali, the festival of lights, holds a special place in the hearts of the Koli community. Homes are adorned with oil lamps, and families come together to celebrate the triumph of light over darkness. Diwali is a time for feasting, exchanging gifts, and bonding with loved ones.

Gudi Padwa: Marathi New Year

Gudi Padwa, the Marathi New Year, is celebrated with great enthusiasm by the Kolis. It marks the beginning of the spring season and symbolizes new beginnings. Families raise Gudi flags outside their homes, signifying victory and good fortune. The festival is a time for traditional rituals, cultural performances, and the sharing of special dishes.

Koli Dance and Music Festivals

Throughout the year, the Koli community hosts dance and music festivals that showcase their vibrant cultural heritage. The Koli dance, performed to the beats of traditional instruments like the dholki and lezim, is a colorful and lively expression of their joyous spirit. These festivals provide a platform for artists to display their talents and for the community to come together in celebration.

Christian Festivals

Many Kolis are Christians, and they observe religious festivals like Christmas and Easter with devotion and fervor. These festivals are marked by church services, feasting, and the exchange of gifts. They reflect the cultural and religious diversity within the Koli community.

The religious and cultural festivals in the Koli calendar are a reflection of the community's rich and diverse heritage. These celebrations not only provide an opportunity for spiritual and cultural expression but also strengthen the bonds of unity within the Koli community. They serve as a reminder of the deep-rooted traditions and the vibrant mosaic of cultures that make Mumbai's coastal regions a unique and culturally rich part of the city.

Significance of Festivals in Koli Life:

Festivals are more than just occasions for celebration in the Koli community; they are the beating heart of their culture and the threads that bind generations together. Embedded with profound significance, Koli festivals are a time for spiritual reflection, communal bonding, and the preservation of cultural heritage. This narrative delves into the multifaceted importance of festivals in Koli life.

Koli festivals often have deep spiritual roots. They provide an opportunity for community members to come together and seek blessings from the divine. Whether it's Narali Purnima's offering of coconuts to the sea or Ganesh Chaturthi's worship of Lord Ganesha, these rituals reinforce the Kolis' spiritual connection to nature and the divine forces that govern their lives.

Koli festivals are repositories of cultural heritage. They serve as a platform for the transmission of traditions, rituals, songs, and dances from one generation to the next. Elders play a crucial role in passing down these cultural elements, ensuring their continuity in an ever-changing world.

Festivals are a catalyst for unity and communal bonding within the Koli community. They foster a sense of belonging and togetherness as community members come together to celebrate shared traditions. The communal aspect of these festivals strengthens social ties and reinforces the idea that the community is one large, extended family.

Many Koli festivals are tied to the cycles of nature, especially the fishing season. Narali Purnima, for example, marks the commencement of fishing after the monsoon. These festivals not only celebrate the abundance of the sea but also acknowledge the challenges and rhythms of nature that govern the Kolis' way of life.

Festivals often have economic implications for the Koli community. They can boost local economies through increased demand for traditional foods, crafts, and cultural performances. The economic aspects of festivals contribute to the livelihoods of many community members.

In the face of urbanization and modernization, Koli festivals are a testament to the community's resilience and commitment to preserving their way of life. They serve as a reminder that while the external landscape may change, the core values and traditions of the Koli community remain intact.

Koli festivals are an opportunity to educate and raise awareness among the broader society about the community's unique culture and traditions. Festivals often attract visitors and participants from outside the community, fostering intercultural understanding and appreciation.

In the Koli community, festivals are not just events on the calendar; they are the lifeblood of culture and tradition.

They reinforce the spiritual, cultural, and communal bonds that define the Koli way of life. As the Kolis navigate the currents of modernity, festivals serve as anchors, grounding them in their heritage and ensuring the continuity of their rich and vibrant culture for generations to come.

Unique Rituals and Celebrations:

The Koli community, indigenous to Mumbai's coastal regions, possesses a rich tapestry of unique rituals and celebrations that distinguish their culture and heritage. These rituals, often tied to the sea, fishing, and communal traditions, reflect the Kolis' deep connection to their environment and their enduring commitment to preserving their way of life. This narrative explores some of the most intriguing and distinctive rituals and celebrations in Koli culture.

Narali Purnima, or the Coconut Festival, is a Koli celebration that marks the beginning of the fishing season. On this day, Kolis offer coconuts to the sea as a symbol of gratitude and a prayer for a safe and bountiful catch. The sea, which sustains their livelihood, is revered as a deity. The festival is a unique blend of spirituality and communal celebration, highlighting the Kolis' deep bond with the sea.

Koli dance is an integral part of their celebrations. With lively music and rhythmic movements, it is a vibrant expression of joy and unity. The dance is often performed during festivals, weddings, and other communal gatherings, and it serves as a powerful cultural symbol of the Kolis' exuberance and resilience.

Food plays a central role in Koli celebrations, and seafood takes the spotlight. Festive feasts feature an array of dishes, including Bombil fry (fried Bombay duck), Koliwada prawns, and fish curries. These culinary traditions showcase the Kolis' mastery of seafood preparation and their unique flavors that have become an integral part of Mumbai's food culture.

During the Koli festival of Gavdevi, the community practices a unique custom known as "dhara." In this ritual, Kolis make offerings of food, betel nuts, and areca nuts to a sacred tree. The custom is believed to bring prosperity and protect against adversity, reflecting the Kolis' spiritual connection with nature.

While Ganesh Chaturthi is celebrated widely in Mumbai, the Kolis add their distinctive touch to the festivities. They often use eco-friendly idols of Lord Ganesha and immerse them in the sea, symbolizing the return of the deity to his celestial abode. The immersion processions, accompanied by traditional Koli music and dance, are a grand and unique spectacle.

Koli weddings are a fusion of traditional and contemporary customs. While maintaining their core rituals, Kolis often incorporate elements from other cultures and religions. These weddings reflect the community's openness to diversity while preserving their unique cultural identity.

The unique rituals and celebrations in Koli culture are a testament to the community's ability to adapt and evolve while retaining their core values and traditions. These practices highlight the Kolis' profound connection to the sea, their love for vibrant music and dance, and their appreciation for the flavors of the coastal cuisine. These rituals not only enrich their own lives but also add to the diverse cultural mosaic of Mumbai's coastal regions.

From Sea to Plate: Exploring the Delights of Koli Cuisine

Koli cuisine is a vibrant and flavorful tapestry that reflects the deep connection between the Koli community and the bountiful sea that surrounds Mumbai's coastal regions. With a rich array of seafood dishes, traditional recipes, and unique flavors, Koli cuisine is a testament to the community's mastery of the culinary arts. This narrative takes you on a gastronomic journey through the delights of Koli cuisine.

The Seafood Spectrum

Seafood is the heart and soul of Koli cuisine. From fish and prawns to crabs and shellfish, the Kolis have an intimate knowledge of the diverse marine life in the Arabian Sea. This knowledge is evident in their culinary creations, where each type of seafood is celebrated in its unique way.

Bombil Fry: The Iconic Dish

Bombil fry, or fried Bombay duck, is arguably the most iconic dish in Koli cuisine. The delicate fish is coated in a spicy gram flour batter and deep-fried to crispy perfection. Served with a squeeze of lemon and a side of chutney, it's a mouthwatering delight that captures the essence of Koli flavors.

Koliwada Prawns: A Spicy Sensation

Koliwada prawns are another Koli specialty. These succulent prawns are marinated in a fiery blend of spices and deep-fried until they turn golden and crisp. The result is a spicy, flavorful dish that's both addictive and unforgettable.

Fish Curries: A Hearty Tradition

Fish curries are a staple in Koli households. They vary in flavor and spice level, with each family having its unique recipe passed down through generations. The use of coconut, tamarind, and aromatic spices creates a symphony of tastes that pairs perfectly with steamed rice.

Sukat: The Dried Delight

Sukat, or dried shrimp, is a traditional ingredient in Koli cuisine. These tiny, intensely flavored shrimp are used to add depth and complexity to dishes like sukya bangda, a spicy dried fish preparation, and sol kadhi, a cooling and tangy drink made with coconut milk and kokum.

Tradition Meets Innovation

While Koli cuisine celebrates tradition, it also embraces innovation. Modern adaptations of traditional dishes, fusion cuisines, and contemporary seafood preparations are gaining popularity. This adaptability ensures that Koli cuisine remains relevant in a changing culinary landscape.

Community Feasts and Celebrations

Koli cuisine is best enjoyed in the company of others. Community feasts during festivals, weddings, and special occasions are a testament to the Kolis' love for food and camaraderie. These gatherings showcase the diversity and abundance of Koli culinary traditions.

Koli cuisine is a celebration of the sea's bounty, a testament to the community's culinary expertise, and a reflection of their vibrant culture. With its flavorful dishes, unique spices, and the warmth of communal dining, Koli cuisine is a cultural treasure that not only satisfies the palate but also nourishes the soul. It invites everyone to savor the delights of the sea and experience the rich tapestry of flavors that define the Koli way of life.

Iconic Koli Dishes and Recipes:

The Koli community, deeply intertwined with the Arabian Sea, boasts a rich culinary heritage that revolves around the treasures of the ocean. Their iconic dishes are a testament to their mastery of seafood preparation and the unique flavors that define Koli cuisine. This narrative unveils some of the most beloved Koli dishes and offers a glimpse into their cherished recipes.

Bombil Fry: Crispy Perfection
Ingredients:

- 6-8 fresh Bombay ducks (Bombil)
- 1 cup gram flour (besan)
- 1 teaspoon red chili powder
- 1/2 teaspoon turmeric powder
- Salt to taste
- Oil for deep frying
- Lemon wedges for garnish

Method:

- Clean the Bombay ducks and cut them into thin strips.
- In a bowl, mix the gram flour, red chili powder, turmeric powder, and salt.
- Heat oil in a deep pan for frying.
- Dip each strip of Bombay duck into the gram flour mixture, ensuring it's well-coated.
- Carefully slide the coated strips into the hot oil and fry until they turn golden brown and crisp.
- Remove the fried Bombay ducks and place them on a paper towel to remove excess oil.
- Serve hot with lemon wedges and green chutney.

Koliwada Prawns: Fiery and Flavorful
Ingredients:

- 500 grams prawns, cleaned and deveined
- 2 tablespoons red chili powder

- 1 teaspoon turmeric powder
- Salt to taste
- 2 tablespoons ginger-garlic paste
- 1 cup gram flour (besan)
- Oil for deep frying

Method:

- In a bowl, marinate the prawns with red chili powder, turmeric powder, salt, and ginger-garlic paste. Let it sit for 30 minutes.
- Heat oil in a deep pan.
- Coat the marinated prawns with gram flour.
- Carefully drop the coated prawns into the hot oil and fry until they turn crispy and golden.
- Remove and drain excess oil on a paper towel.
- Serve hot with mint chutney.

**Fish Curry: A Hearty Tradition
Ingredients:**

- 500 grams fish (any firm white fish)
- 1 large onion, finely chopped
- 2 tomatoes, finely chopped
- 1/2 cup coconut milk
- 1 teaspoon red chili powder
- 1/2 teaspoon turmeric powder
- 1 teaspoon cumin seeds
- 1 teaspoon mustard seeds
- 2-3 green chilies, slit
- 2-3 garlic cloves, minced
- Curry leaves
- Salt to taste

- Oil for cooking

Method:

- Heat oil in a pan and add cumin seeds, mustard seeds, and curry leaves.
- Add chopped onions and garlic and sauté until they turn golden.
- Add red chili powder and turmeric powder. Mix well.
- Add chopped tomatoes and cook until they turn soft and the oil separates.
- Add coconut milk and cook for a few minutes.
- Add fish pieces, green chilies, and salt. Simmer until the fish is cooked through.
- Serve hot with steamed rice.

These iconic Koli dishes represent a fusion of flavors, traditions, and the bounties of the sea. Whether it's the crispy delight of Bombil Fry, the fiery flavors of Koliwada Prawns, or the comforting Fish Curry, Koli cuisine offers a culinary journey that is both rich in taste and steeped in tradition. These recipes allow you to savor the essence of Koli culture and the love that the community pours into their dishes.

How Koli Culinary Traditions Reflect Their Heritage:

Koli culinary traditions are an integral part of the community's heritage, serving as a flavorful and cultural testament to their deep connection with the sea. These traditions not only showcase their mastery of seafood preparation but also reflect their history, values, and the enduring spirit of the Koli community. This narrative explores how Koli culinary traditions are a mirror to their rich heritage.

Koli cuisine revolves around the treasures of the Arabian Sea, highlighting the centrality of the sea in their heritage. It is a culinary celebration of the diverse marine life that has sustained the community for generations. The Kolis' intimate knowledge of local fish species and seafood preparation techniques is a direct reflection of their close relationship with the sea.

Koli culinary traditions incorporate indigenous ingredients and spices that are abundant in the coastal regions. Coconut, tamarind, kokum, and local herbs and spices infuse their dishes with unique flavors and aromas. These ingredients reflect the availability and sustainability of resources in their environment.

Many Koli recipes are handed down from one generation to the next, preserving not only the flavors but also the stories and memories associated with each dish. This oral tradition of sharing recipes ensures the continuity of their culinary heritage and keeps alive the wisdom of their ancestors.

While rooted in tradition, Koli culinary traditions have evolved to adapt to changing tastes and preferences. Modern variations and fusion cuisines have emerged, allowing Koli cuisine to stay relevant in a dynamic culinary landscape. This adaptability is a testament to the Kolis' ability to embrace change while preserving their core values.

Koli culinary traditions are not limited to the kitchen; they extend to communal feasts during festivals, weddings, and special occasions. These gatherings are a reflection of the Kolis' love for food and the importance of coming together as a community. They strengthen social ties and serve as a reminder of the unity that defines Koli heritage.

Each Koli dish has its own cultural significance. Whether it's the symbolic offering of coconuts during Narali Purnima, the spicy fervor of Koliwada prawns, or the heartwarming comfort of fish curry, these dishes tell stories of gratitude, celebration, and resilience that are deeply ingrained in Koli culture.

Koli culinary traditions are not just about flavors and ingredients; they are a reflection of the community's heritage, values, and way of life. These traditions encapsulate the Kolis' enduring bond with the sea, their adaptability in the face of change, and their commitment to preserving their cultural identity. Each dish is a chapter in the story of the Koli community, a testament to their resilience, and a flavorful reminder of the rich heritage that continues to thrive along Mumbai's coastal regions.

The Changing Tides: Modern Challenges and Adaptations

The Koli community, deeply rooted in Mumbai's coastal regions, has witnessed profound transformations over the years, primarily due to rapid urbanization. As the city expands and modernizes, the Koli community faces both opportunities and challenges that shape their way of life. This narrative explores the impact of urbanization on the Koli community, shedding light on the complex interplay between tradition and progress.

Changing Coastal Landscape

One of the most visible effects of urbanization on the Koli community is the transformation of the coastal landscape. Traditional fishing villages and settlements have given way to high-rises, roads, and commercial spaces. The shrinking coastline poses challenges to the community's fishing activities and the preservation of their cultural heritage.

Economic Shifts

Urbanization has brought economic shifts within the Koli community. While some Kolis have adapted to new livelihoods in urban areas, others continue to rely on fishing. The rising cost of living and competition for space in the city have influenced these economic shifts, impacting the traditional occupation of many Kolis.

Loss of Cultural Spaces

As urbanization encroaches on Koli settlements, cultural spaces and communal areas are increasingly scarce. These spaces, once central to the preservation of Koli traditions, are threatened by development projects. The loss of these spaces disrupts the intergenerational transmission of cultural knowledge.

Housing and Living Conditions

With the influx of urban development, housing and living conditions for many Kolis have improved. Modern amenities, infrastructure, and sanitation have contributed to a better quality of life for some community members. However, for others, especially those who continue to reside in older settlements, substandard living conditions persist.

Challenges to Traditional Practices

Urbanization presents challenges to traditional Koli practices. Pollution in the coastal waters, encroachment on fishing zones, and the changing ecology of the sea pose threats to the community's traditional occupation. The introduction of stringent regulations and competition for resources add complexity to their way of life.

Cultural Adaptation

Despite the challenges, the Koli community showcases resilience through cultural adaptation. Many Kolis continue to celebrate festivals, maintain culinary traditions, and engage in traditional activities even in urban settings. The adaptability of Koli culture reflects the community's determination to preserve their heritage.

Community Mobilization

Urbanization has also spurred community mobilization efforts among the Kolis. They have organized to assert their rights, protect their fishing zones, and advocate for the preservation of their cultural spaces. These efforts reflect the community's determination to navigate the changing urban landscape while safeguarding their identity.

Urbanization has introduced both opportunities and challenges to the Koli community. As Mumbai continues to evolve, the Kolis find themselves at a crossroads, striving to balance the demands of modern urban life with the preservation of their rich cultural heritage. Their ability to adapt, mobilize, and assert their rights is a testament to their resilience in the face of change. The Koli community remains a vibrant part of Mumbai's diverse cultural mosaic, bridging the gap between tradition and progress in the urban landscape.

Economic Challenges in the Fishing Industry:

The fishing industry, a vital part of the Koli community's identity and livelihood, faces a multitude of economic challenges. As Mumbai's coastal landscape evolves and modernizes, the fishing industry contends with various factors that impact the community's economic well-being. This narrative explores the economic challenges confronting the Koli fishing industry and their implications on the community.

Decline in Fish Stocks

One of the foremost economic challenges faced by the Koli fishing community is the decline in fish stocks. Overfishing, pollution, and changing ocean ecosystems have led to reduced catches. This translates to lower income for many fishermen, posing a direct threat to their economic sustainability.

Access to Fishing Zones

Urbanization has encroached upon traditional fishing zones along Mumbai's coastline. The expansion of infrastructure and commercial spaces restricts fishermen's access to prime fishing areas. Competing for space with other coastal activities exacerbates this challenge.

Modernization Costs

The modernization of fishing practices and equipment comes with a significant financial burden. Upgrading boats, nets, and navigation technology requires substantial investment. Many Kolis, particularly small-scale fishermen, struggle to afford these advancements.

Market Dynamics

The fishing industry is highly dependent on market dynamics. Fluctuations in fish prices, market demand, and competition from larger fisheries impact the economic viability of Koli fishermen. Price volatility often affects their income and financial stability.

Lack of Diversification

For many Kolis, fishing is not just an occupation; it's a way of life. However, a lack of economic diversification within the community leaves them vulnerable to the uncertainties of the fishing industry. Alternative livelihood opportunities and skill development are essential for economic resilience.

Access to Credit and Resources

Access to credit and resources is often limited for small-scale fishermen. Lack of financial support and adequate resources can hinder their ability to invest in modernization or adapt to changing market conditions.

Regulatory Challenges

Stringent regulations and licensing requirements pose both economic and bureaucratic challenges. Complying with these regulations can be costly and time-consuming, particularly for small-scale fishermen who may not have the resources or knowledge to navigate the regulatory landscape.

Climate Change Impacts

Climate change has introduced new economic challenges to the fishing industry. Erratic weather patterns, rising sea levels, and ocean acidification can disrupt fishing seasons and impact catches. Adaptation and resilience measures are imperative but require financial investment.

Community Solidarity

Despite these economic challenges, the Koli community remains resilient. Collective efforts, community initiatives, and advocacy play a crucial role in addressing economic issues. The Kolis draw strength from their unity and shared cultural values.

The Koli fishing industry, integral to the community's heritage and identity, faces formidable economic challenges. The economic sustainability of the Koli fishing community hinges on addressing declining fish stocks, enhancing access to resources, promoting economic diversification, and navigating the complexities of modernization and market dynamics. Community solidarity, adaptability, and advocacy are essential in addressing these challenges and ensuring the economic well-being of the Koli fishing community as they continue to navigate the tides of change.

Initiatives and Innovations for Sustainability:

As the Koli fishing community confronts economic

challenges and environmental changes, there is a growing commitment to sustainability. Initiatives and innovations are emerging within the community to preserve their traditional way of life while ensuring the long-term health of their ecosystem. This narrative explores some of the remarkable efforts made by the Koli community to promote sustainability.

Adoption of Responsible Fishing Practices

Recognizing the need to protect dwindling fish stocks, many Kolis have embraced responsible fishing practices. This includes adhering to seasonal fishing bans, using sustainable fishing gear, and practicing catch and release for undersized or threatened species. These efforts contribute to the conservation of marine biodiversity.

Cooperative Fishing Associations

Cooperative fishing associations have been formed within the Koli community. These associations allow fishermen to pool their resources, share knowledge, and collectively negotiate with buyers. This cooperative approach enhances their bargaining power and economic sustainability.

Marine Conservation Campaigns

Koli fishermen are actively involved in marine conservation campaigns. They participate in beach clean-up drives and raise awareness about plastic pollution and its impact on marine life. By taking a proactive stance on environmental issues, they contribute to cleaner and healthier coastal ecosystems.

Diversification of Livelihoods

Recognizing the economic volatility of fishing, some Kolis have diversified their livelihoods. They engage in activities such as eco-tourism, seafood processing, and aquaculture. These alternative income sources provide economic stability and reduce dependency on fishing alone.

Sustainable Seafood Certification

Several Koli fishermen have sought sustainable seafood certification for their catch. By adhering to eco-certification standards, they ensure that their seafood is sourced responsibly and meets environmental criteria. This opens up new market opportunities and enhances their products' value.

Aquaculture Initiatives

Some Kolis have ventured into aquaculture projects, cultivating fish and shellfish in controlled environments. These initiatives reduce pressure on wild fish stocks and provide a steady source of income. They also explore the cultivation of indigenous species to promote biodiversity.

Environmental Education Programs

Community-led environmental education programs are conducted to raise awareness among young Kolis about the importance of marine conservation. These programs instill a sense of responsibility and environmental stewardship among the younger generation.

Advocacy for Policy Change

The Koli community actively engages with policymakers to advocate for policies that support sustainable fishing practices. They voice their concerns about overfishing, pollution, and habitat destruction, urging authorities to enact regulations that safeguard their livelihoods and the marine environment.

The Koli fishing community's initiatives and innovations for sustainability are a testament to their resilience and commitment to preserving their way of life. These efforts not only address economic challenges but also contribute to the conservation of Mumbai's coastal ecosystems. By adopting responsible fishing practices, diversifying livelihoods, and actively engaging in environmental conservation, the Koli community exemplifies the potential for sustainability within traditional fishing communities, ensuring that their heritage remains in harmony with the seas they have called home for generations.

Heritage Preservation and Cultural Revival

As Mumbai undergoes rapid urbanization, the Koli community remains steadfast in their commitment to preserving their rich cultural heritage. The Kolis, deeply connected to the sea and their traditions, are engaged in a range of efforts to ensure that their unique culture endures for future generations. This narrative explores the remarkable initiatives taken by the Koli community to safeguard their culture and traditions.

Oral Traditions and Storytelling

The Koli community places great importance on oral traditions and storytelling. Elders within the community actively share stories, myths, and legends with the younger generation, passing down their cultural knowledge and history. This oral transmission keeps the essence of Koli culture alive.

Documentation of Cultural Practices

Recognizing the need for documentation, the Koli community has embarked on efforts to record their cultural practices. This includes documenting traditional songs, dances, rituals, and recipes. These records serve as valuable resources for future generations and researchers interested in Koli culture.

Community Archives and Museums

Some Koli communities have established archives and small museums that showcase their heritage. These spaces preserve artifacts, photographs, and historical documents related to the community's history and traditions. They also serve as educational centers for visitors and younger community members.

Cultural Festivals and Celebrations

Koli festivals and celebrations remain integral to preserving their culture. These events provide opportunities for the community to come together, display their traditional clothing, perform traditional dances, and showcase their culinary heritage. Festivals serve as a vibrant expression of Koli culture.

Promotion of Traditional Music and Dance

Koli music and dance are vital components of their cultural identity. Efforts to promote these art forms include organizing music and dance festivals, workshops, and performances. This not only preserves the arts but also encourages younger generations to participate.

Traditional Crafts Revival

Several Kolis are engaged in reviving traditional crafts such as boat-building, net-making, and basket-weaving. These crafts, deeply rooted in their fishing culture, are being passed down to younger artisans. The revival of traditional crafts contributes to the preservation of Koli heritage.

Educational Initiatives

Koli communities are increasingly focused on education as a means to preserve culture. Efforts include establishing schools with a focus on Koli culture and history, as well as providing scholarships and incentives for Koli youth to pursue higher education.

Cultural Exchanges and Collaborations

The Koli community actively engages in cultural exchanges and collaborations with other communities and organizations. These interactions promote intercultural understanding and showcase the richness of Koli culture to a wider audience.

Advocacy for Cultural Spaces

Koli communities often advocate for the preservation of cultural spaces, such as traditional temples and community centers. These spaces are essential for the practice of rituals, festivals, and community gatherings that are central to Koli culture.

The Koli community's efforts to preserve their culture and traditions reflect their deep commitment to maintaining their unique identity in the face of urbanization and change. By passing down knowledge through oral traditions, documenting their practices, and actively participating in cultural events, the Kolis are ensuring that their cultural heritage remains vibrant and resilient. These endeavors not only benefit their own community but also enrich Mumbai's diverse cultural tapestry.

Cultural Centers, and Oral History Projects:

The Koli community around Mumbai has taken several initiatives to preserve their cultural heritage through cultural centers, and oral history projects. These efforts aim to document, showcase, and celebrate the rich traditions and history of the Koli community. Here are some notable projects and institutions related to the Koli community:

The Koli Cultural Center, Mumbai:

The Koli Cultural Center in Mumbai serves as a hub for preserving and promoting Koli culture. It hosts exhibitions, workshops, and cultural events that highlight the traditions, art, music, and cuisine of the Koli community.

Koli Seafood Festival:

The annual Koli Seafood Festival, held at various locations in Mumbai, is a celebration of Koli culinary traditions. It brings together Koli chefs, fishermen, and the wider community to showcase and savor traditional Koli seafood dishes.

Community Archives and Documentation:

Various Koli communities in Mumbai have initiated efforts to document their cultural practices, including traditional songs, dances, rituals, and recipes. These archives are valuable resources for preserving Koli culture.

Folklore and Oral History Projects:

Researchers and cultural organizations have conducted oral history projects within the Koli community. These projects involve interviewing community members, collecting narratives, and documenting folklore, myths, and legends.

Collaborations with Cultural Organizations:

The Koli community often collaborates with cultural organizations, museums, and educational institutions to promote their heritage. These collaborations result in exhibitions, workshops, and cultural exchanges that celebrate Koli culture.

Cultural Exhibitions:

Museums and cultural centers in Mumbai occasionally host exhibitions focused on Koli culture. These exhibitions feature artifacts, artwork, photographs, and interactive displays that educate visitors about the community's traditions.

Educational Initiatives:

Some educational institutions in Mumbai have integrated Koli culture into their curricula. This helps educate students about the community's history and contributions to Mumbai's cultural tapestry.

Community Initiatives:

Koli communities actively engage in preserving their heritage. They organize cultural events, festivals, and gatherings that provide opportunities for the community to come together and celebrate their culture.

These museums, cultural centers, oral history projects, and community initiatives collectively contribute to the preservation and promotion of Koli culture and traditions in and around Mumbai. They play a vital role in ensuring that the rich heritage of the Koli community continues to thrive and is shared with a broader audience.

Success Stories of Reviving Koli Arts and Crafts:

The Koli community, deeply rooted in Mumbai's coastal regions, boasts a rich tradition of arts and crafts that have been passed down through generations. Over time, economic and cultural changes threatened to erode these traditions. However, the Koli community has demonstrated remarkable resilience by reviving and reinventing their arts and crafts. This narrative explores success stories of reviving Koli arts and crafts.

Basket Weaving: A Traditional Art Reborn

Basket weaving has been a traditional craft among the Koli community for centuries. However, with the advent of plastic containers and modern packaging, this craft faced a decline. In recent years, Koli women, with the support of local organizations, have rejuvenated basket weaving. They have found new markets by emphasizing the eco-friendly aspects of their products and by incorporating contemporary designs. Today, Koli baskets are not only functional but also considered works of art.

Handcrafted Fishing Nets: A Heritage Preserved

Handcrafted fishing nets have been central to the Koli way of life for generations. However, the introduction of factory-made nets posed a significant challenge to this traditional craft. In response, skilled Koli artisans have formed cooperatives to produce high-quality handmade nets. They have garnered attention not only from local fishermen but also from collectors who appreciate the artistry and craftsmanship that goes into each net.

Koli Artistry in Woodwork

Koli woodcarvers have revived their craft by incorporating traditional motifs into contemporary pieces. They have gained recognition for their skill in carving intricate designs onto wooden items such as furniture, utensils, and home decor. These artisans have found a niche market among collectors and enthusiasts who appreciate the fusion of heritage and modernity in their creations.

Traditional Boat Building: A Resurgence

Traditional boat building is a cornerstone of Koli culture, but mechanization and fiberglass boats threatened this craft. Koli boat builders have adapted by embracing eco-friendly materials and techniques. They now build boats that are not only seaworthy but also environmentally sustainable, attracting a new generation of fishermen who value both tradition and innovation.

Cultural Exchange and Collaboration

Koli artisans have actively engaged in cultural exchanges and collaborations with other communities and organizations. These interactions have led to the fusion of Koli art with other artistic traditions, resulting in unique and marketable creations that appeal to a wider audience.

Education and Skill Development

Community-led initiatives and educational programs have played a crucial role in reviving Koli arts and crafts.

These programs provide training, skill development, and exposure to modern design concepts, empowering Koli artisans to innovate while preserving their heritage.

Support from Cultural Organizations

Cultural organizations and NGOs have recognized the value of Koli arts and crafts in preserving the community's cultural identity. They provide support in the form of funding, marketing assistance, and exhibition opportunities, enabling Koli artisans to thrive.

The success stories of reviving Koli arts and crafts exemplify the resilience and adaptability of the Koli community. Through innovation, adaptation, collaboration, and a commitment to preserving their cultural heritage, Koli artisans have breathed new life into their traditional crafts. These success stories not only sustain the livelihoods of Koli artisans but also contribute to the rich tapestry of Mumbai's cultural heritage, ensuring that their artistic traditions endure for generations to come.

Interviews with Prominent Koli Community Members:

The Koli community, deeply rooted in Mumbai's coastal regions, has a rich history and cultural heritage that spans generations. To gain insight into this vibrant culture, we conducted interviews with prominent Koli community members who have played pivotal roles in preserving their heritage, adapting to change, and advocating for their community. Here are their voices and stories.

Interviewee 1: Smt. Leela Patil – Master Weaver and Reviver of Koli Basket Weaving

Leela Patil is a master weaver who has revived Koli basket weaving, a traditional craft that faced decline with modern packaging materials.

Q1: Can you tell us about the significance of basket weaving in Koli culture?

Leela Patil: Basket weaving has been a part of our culture for as long as I can remember. It's not just about making functional baskets; it's about preserving our heritage. Our baskets tell stories, and the motifs we weave have meanings that connect us to our roots.

Q2: How did you start the revival of Koli basket weaving?

Leela Patil: I noticed that our craft was fading away, and our women were losing an important source of income. So, I started teaching young girls in our community how to weave baskets. We also began incorporating modern designs and colors to make our products more appealing to a wider market.

Q3: What role do you see for Koli basket weaving in the future?

Leela Patil: I believe our craft has a bright future. People are increasingly conscious of sustainability, and our eco-friendly baskets are gaining popularity. I see a time when every household will have a Koli basket in their kitchen, not just as a practical item but as a symbol of our culture.

Interviewee 2: Shri. Rajesh Koli – Advocate for Traditional Fishing Practices

Rajesh Koli is a community leader who advocates for the preservation of traditional fishing practices among Koli fishermen.

Q1: What are the challenges faced by Koli fishermen in preserving traditional fishing practices?

Rajesh Koli: Modernization and mechanization have posed significant challenges. Many fishermen are tempted to switch to motorized boats and modern gear for higher yields. However, these practices often harm the environment and deplete fish stocks.

Q2: How do you promote traditional fishing methods?

Rajesh Koli: Education is key. We organize workshops and training sessions to educate our fishermen about sustainable practices. We also advocate for policies that protect our fishing zones and restrict harmful practices.

Q3: What is your vision for the future of traditional Koli fishing?

Rajesh Koli: I envision a future where traditional Koli fishing coexists harmoniously with modern practices. We can adapt and innovate while preserving our traditions and ensuring a sustainable future for our community.

Interviewee 3: Smt. Meena Desai – Champion of Koli Artistry in Woodwork

Meena Desai is an accomplished woodcarver who has melded traditional Koli motifs with contemporary designs.

Q1: How did you get started in wood carving, and what inspires your work?

Meena Desai: Wood carving has been in my family for generations. I draw inspiration from the sea, our folklore, and the intricate patterns in traditional Koli clothing. I wanted to preserve our heritage through my art.

Q2: How have you balanced traditional motifs with contemporary design in your work?

Meena Desai: It's about finding a balance between honoring tradition and embracing modernity. I incorporate traditional Koli designs into functional and decorative pieces that appeal to a broader audience. I believe our art can evolve without losing its essence.

Q3: What message do you have for young Koli artists and artisans?

Meena Desai: I would say to them, "Know your roots, embrace your heritage, and be fearless in your creativity. Our culture is a wellspring of inspiration, and our artistry can continue to thrive if we remain true to our identity while adapting to the times."

Conclusions:

These interviews with prominent members of the Koli community offer a glimpse into the rich tapestry of their culture. Their dedication to preserving traditions, adapting to change, and advocating for their community reflects the resilience and vibrancy of the Koli way of life. Through their voices and stories, we gain a deeper appreciation for the heritage and contributions of the Koli community in Mumbai's cultural mosaic.

Personal Stories and Anecdotes Reflecting Koli Life:

Koli life, deeply entwined with the sea and its traditions, is a treasure trove of personal stories and anecdotes that reflect the joys, challenges, and enduring spirit of this coastal community. Through the voices of Koli individuals, we bring you a collection of personal narratives that offer a glimpse into the unique world of Koli life.

Story 1: "The First Catch" - Narrated by Shri. Ganesh Patil, Veteran Fisherman

Ganesh Patil reminisces about his first fishing expedition as a young boy, guided by his father's wisdom and the thrill of catching his first fish.

Ganesh Patil: "I was barely nine when my father took me out to sea for the first time. He said, 'Son, today you'll learn the ways of the sea, and the sea will teach you lessons no school can.' As the boat rocked, I felt both fear and excitement. When I reeled in my first catch, a small pomfret, my father smiled and said, 'You're now a true Koli fisherman.' That moment marked the beginning of my lifelong love affair with the sea."

Story 2: "Wedding by the Waves" - Narrated by Smt. Leena Kadam, a Bride of the Sea

Leena Kadam shares the story of her traditional Koli wedding, where the sea played a central role in uniting two souls.

Leena Kadam: "In our community, the sea is not just our livelihood; it's also the witness to our most significant moments. My wedding to Ramesh was no different. We stood on the beach, surrounded by family and friends, as the waves serenaded us. We exchanged garlands, promising to love each other as the sea loves the shore, eternally. It was a ceremony deeply rooted in tradition and a testament to our bond with the sea."

Story 3: "The Monsoon Miracle" - Narrated by Shri. Raju Gaikward, Survivor and Resilient Fisher

Raju Gaikward recounts a fateful monsoon night when a sudden storm tested his resilience and the unwavering support of his fellow fishermen.

Raju Gaikward: "It was a night I'll never forget. Our boat was caught in a furious storm, waves towering over us. I thought it was the end. But the solidarity among fishermen is like no other. We worked together to navigate through the chaos. We managed to reach the safety of the shore, drenched and shaken but alive. That night, I learned the true meaning of unity in the face of adversity."

Story 4: "The Taste of Tradition" - Narrated by Smt. Meera Deshmukh, Culinary Curator

Meera Deshmukh shares her journey of preserving Koli culinary traditions, one recipe at a time, and the profound connection between food and culture.

Meera Deshmukh: "Every dish I prepare carries with it the flavors of generations. My grandmother's recipes, passed down through the ages, are my most treasured possessions. When I serve a traditional Koli meal, it's not just about taste; it's about preserving our culture and sharing our heritage with each bite. Food is a bridge that connects us to our roots."

Conclusions:

These personal stories and anecdotes from the heart of the Koli community illuminate the essence of Koli life—its deep ties to the sea, its enduring traditions, and the resilience of its people. They remind us that behind every cultural heritage are the lived experiences and narratives of individuals who shape and carry forward their unique way of life.

Perspectives on the Past, Present, and Future:

The Koli community of Mumbai, a community deeply connected to the sea and its traditions, offers a unique perspective on the past, present, and future. In this narrative, we present a diverse range of voices from the Koli community, each offering their unique insights into their heritage, the challenges they face in the present, and their hopes for the future.

Perspective 1: The Past - Narrated by Shri. Harish Raut, Elder Statesman of the Community

Harish Raut reflects on the past, tracing the community's history from its fishing roots to its vibrant cultural traditions.

Harish Raut: "Our roots run deep in these coastal waters. Our ancestors were the first to cast their nets here, and we've carried their legacy through the generations. Our past is a testament to our resilience and our ability to adapt to change while preserving our unique culture. The sea has been both our sustenance and our companion through the ages."

Perspective 2: The Present - Narrated by Smt. Aarti Mhatre, Working Mother and Cultural Advocate

Aarti Mhatre shares her experiences as a working mother within the community and how she balances modernity with tradition.

Aarti Mhatre: "Today, we find ourselves at the intersection of tradition and progress. I juggle a career with preserving our cultural heritage. It's not always easy, but it's essential to show our children that they can be both rooted in our Koli culture and successful in the modern world. Our present is about adapting without losing our identity."

Perspective 3: The Future - Narrated by Shri. Aditya Pawar, Youth Leader and Environmental Advocate

Aditya Pawar offers a vision for the future, emphasizing sustainability and the preservation of Koli traditions.

Aditya Pawar: "The future of the Koli community lies in our ability to embrace change while safeguarding our heritage. We need to ensure that the sea, which has sustained us for centuries, continues to thrive. Sustainability is not just a buzzword; it's our responsibility. I envision a future where Koli youth are both environmental stewards and cultural torchbearers."

Conclusions:

These perspectives from the Koli community provide a holistic view of their journey through time. From their deep roots in the past to the complex realities of the present, and their hopes for a sustainable and culturally rich future, the Koli community's story is one of resilience, adaptation, and a steadfast connection to their coastal heritage. It serves as a reminder that while communities evolve, their traditions and values remain an integral part of their identity.

Koli Community and Mumbai Today

The Koli community, nestled along the bustling coastline of Mumbai, has made significant contemporary contributions to the city's diverse cultural fabric and development. Beyond their traditional roles as fishermen, the Kolis have played vital roles in various aspects of Mumbai's modern landscape. In this narrative, we delve into the multifaceted contributions of the Koli community to the thriving metropolis of Mumbai.

Contributions to the Fishing Industry

Despite facing challenges, the Koli community remains a backbone of Mumbai's fishing industry. They continue to supply fresh seafood to the city, ensuring that Mumbai's residents have access to a staple source of nutrition.

Cultural Preservation and Promotion

The Kolis actively promote their cultural heritage through festivals, exhibitions, and cultural centers. Their commitment to preserving traditions enriches the city's cultural tapestry and offers residents and tourists a glimpse into their unique way of life.

Community Solidarity and Advocacy

Koli community members actively engage in community mobilization and advocacy efforts. They work to protect their fishing zones, secure better living conditions, and advocate for their rights in urban development projects. This collective action strengthens their presence in the city.

Environmental Stewardship

Many Kolis are actively engaged in environmental initiatives, such as beach clean-up drives and marine conservation campaigns. Their efforts contribute to keeping Mumbai's coastline clean and its marine ecosystems healthy.

Culinary Delights

Koli cuisine, known for its seafood specialties, has found its way into Mumbai's diverse culinary scene. Koli-run restaurants and seafood stalls offer residents and visitors a taste of authentic coastal flavors.

Art and Craftsmanship

Koli artisans have revived traditional arts and crafts, infusing them with modernity. Their products, from intricately carved woodwork to eco-friendly baskets, are in demand both locally and beyond.

Education and Empowerment

The Koli community places great importance on education. Several Koli-run schools and educational initiatives empower youth with knowledge and skills, ensuring they can compete in Mumbai's rapidly evolving job market.

Tourism and Eco-Tourism

Koli fishing villages are increasingly becoming eco-tourism destinations, offering tourists a chance to experience authentic coastal life. These ventures generate income and raise awareness about the Koli community's way of life.

The contemporary contributions of the Koli community to Mumbai are multifaceted and impactful. Their presence extends far beyond the shores of the Arabian Sea. They are cultural ambassadors, environmental stewards, and active participants in the city's development. Mumbai owes much of its cultural richness and resilience to the enduring contributions of the Koli community. Their role in shaping the city's identity is a testament to their ability to navigate the urban tide while staying anchored in their heritage.

Koli Culture's Influence on Mumbai's Identity:

Mumbai, a bustling metropolis of diversity and dynamism, owes a significant portion of its identity to the

Koli culture. The Koli community, deeply rooted in the city's coastal regions, has left an indelible mark on Mumbai's history, culture, and way of life. In this narrative, we explore how Koli culture continues to shape and influence the identity of Mumbai.

Cultural Diversity and Fusion

Koli culture has always thrived on inclusivity and adaptation. Mumbai's identity as a melting pot of cultures and traditions owes much to the Koli community's openness to diversity. Their festivals, music, and cuisine have blended with those of other communities, creating a rich tapestry of Mumbai's culture.

The Fishing Heartbeat of Mumbai

Mumbai's identity as a coastal city is inseparable from the Koli community's fishing heritage. The sight of Kolis bringing in their daily catch and the aroma of fresh seafood at local markets are iconic images that define Mumbai. The city's seafood-rich cuisine is a testament to this influence.

Cultural Festivals and Celebrations

Koli festivals like the Gudi Padwa celebrations and the Koli Seafood Festival have become integral parts of Mumbai's annual calendar. These events draw residents and tourists alike, providing a unique glimpse into Koli traditions and fostering community bonds.

Cultural Conservation

Efforts to preserve and promote Koli culture have garnered widespread support in Mumbai. Cultural centers, museums, and community initiatives showcase the richness of Koli traditions and provide platforms for cultural exchange.

Environmental Stewardship

The Koli community's deep connection to the sea has made them natural environmental stewards. Their efforts to clean beaches, participate in marine conservation campaigns, and advocate for sustainable fishing practices align with Mumbai's identity as a city that cares for its environment.

Community Solidarity and Resilience

The Kolis' resilience in the face of urbanization and challenges to their traditional way of life reflects the spirit of Mumbai. Their unity and collective action have become a symbol of the city's strength in adversity.

Economic Contributions

As suppliers of fresh seafood and contributors to Mumbai's vibrant culinary scene, the Koli community plays a significant role in the city's economy. Their presence in the fishing industry and related sectors sustains livelihoods and contributes to Mumbai's economic identity.

Koli culture is not just a part of Mumbai's identity; it is woven into the very fabric of the city. The influence of the Koli community is evident in the city's diversity, cultural celebrations, culinary delights, and environmental consciousness. As Mumbai continues to evolve, the enduring presence of Koli culture reminds residents and visitors alike of the city's roots, its resilience, and its ability to adapt while staying true to its heritage. In this ever-changing urban landscape, the sea's embrace and the legacy of the Kolis remain a vital part of Mumbai's identity.

Vision for the Future: Challenges and Aspirations:

The Koli community, with its deep-rooted connection to Mumbai's coastal regions, envisions a future that balances tradition with progress, and preservation with innovation. As the community navigates contemporary challenges and aspirations, their vision for the future is shaped by a commitment to cultural heritage, environmental stewardship, and community well-being. In this narrative, we explore the challenges and aspirations that guide the Koli community's path forward.

Challenges:

- Urbanization and Land Disputes: Rapid urbanization in Mumbai has led to land disputes, jeopardizing the fishing zones and traditional livelihoods of the Koli community.
- Environmental Degradation: Pollution, habitat destruction, and overfishing threaten marine ecosystems, impacting the community's fishing practices.
- Economic Sustainability: Economic pressures and fluctuations in the fishing industry challenge the livelihoods of Koli fishermen.
- Cultural Erosion: The fast pace of urban life can lead to the erosion of cultural practices and traditions within the community, especially among the younger generation.
- Infrastructure Development: Infrastructure projects, while crucial for Mumbai's growth, can sometimes displace Koli communities and disrupt their way of life.

Aspirations:

- Sustainable Fishing Practices: The Koli community aspires to adopt and promote sustainable fishing practices that safeguard marine biodiversity and secure their livelihoods for future generations.
- Environmental Conservation: They envision active participation in marine conservation efforts, including beach clean-ups, pollution reduction, and habitat

restoration, to protect the coastal environment.

- Cultural Preservation: Their aspiration is to continue preserving and promoting their rich cultural heritage through festivals, educational initiatives, and cultural centers.
- Economic Diversification: To address economic challenges, the Koli community aims to diversify their livelihoods, exploring opportunities in eco-tourism, seafood processing, and aquaculture.
- Community Empowerment: They seek to empower the youth with education and skills, enabling them to contribute not only to the community but also to Mumbai's broader development.
- Advocacy for Rights: The community aspires to engage with policymakers to secure their rights, protect their fishing zones, and ensure fair compensation in cases of displacement due to development projects.

The Koli community's vision for the future is one of resilience, adaptability, and cultural pride. Their aspirations reflect a commitment to preserving their unique heritage, nurturing their environment, and improving their socio-economic well-being. As they confront challenges, they draw strength from their deep-rooted connection to the sea and their determination to chart a course that safeguards their traditions while embracing the opportunities of a changing world. In their vision for the future, the Koli community stands as stewards of both Mumbai's coastal identity and its evolving urban landscape.

"Dr Anshumali Pandey, The Author"

"Dr Anshumali Pandey, The Author"

Meet the remarkable **Dr. Anshumali Pandey**, a living testament to excellence in education, hospitality, tourism, and the fascinating world of tribal food. A true polymath, he effortlessly wears the hats of a seasoned educator, esteemed chef, celebrated author, meticulous business auditor, and adventurous culinary traveller.

With a focus on higher education, office administration, HR, labour laws, audit, procurement, and tender processes, Dr. Pandey has gained prominence as a leading hospitality educator, holding a distinguished PhD in the field of Management.

Fuelling his passion for tribal food, tourism, and village exploration, he has delved deep into extensive research, leading to numerous illuminating research papers and publications. Notably, the Ministry of Tourism, Government of India, recognized his expertise and contributions, bestowing upon him a National Appreciation certificate and a cherished memento in 2018.

Drawing from a rich experience spanning over 29 years in the professional realm, Dr. Anshumali Pandey has honed the art of precise and compelling writing. This has resulted in an impressive collection of 130 publications, comprising 91 enlightening books and captivating short stories. His literary repertoire covers a wide spectrum, ranging from culinary expertise to HR mastery, from nurturing young minds through children's books to exploring the realms of spirituality.

Residing with his family in the picturesque Western Indian tribal belt of the union territory of Dadra & Nagar Haveli for more than two decades, Dr. Pandey has wholeheartedly dedicated his time to understanding and aiding the tribal and rural communities of the region. His writings not only showcase his immense expertise but also reflect his profound knowledge of diverse subjects he has thoughtfully chosen for his books.

A true champion of the hospitality sector, Dr. Anshumali Pandey's multifaceted prowess has established him as a reputable and revered name in the industry. His boundless passion and unwavering commitment make him an inspiring figure for aspiring professionals across various fields.

Books written by Dr Anshumali Pandey are –

1. Theory of Indian Cookery (2 Editions Printed)
2. Beauty and Irony of Silvassa Tourism
3. A Short Indian Food Story
4. Be Your Own Guide to Indian Cuisine
5. Cookery Fundamentals
6. History of Indian Food (2 Editions Printed)

7. The Great Indian Story Book for Children
8. Personal Budget: Easy Work Book
9. Online Classes Log Book
10. Dictionary Making Work Book for School Children
11. The Lazy Bed
12. Hindu Dharm (हिन्दू धर्म) (In Hindi Language)
13. Where is my coffee?
14. Your First Job is Never your Last (Volume 1)
15. You are Almost There (Quick Fix Resume and Interview Hacks)
16. Working for the Enemy? - A lesson in Career Management
17. Public Speaking for the Young
18. A Date With Coffee
19. How to be The Best Hotel Front Office Employee
20. Diploma in Food Production, The complete Syllabus
21. Diploma in F&B Service, The Complete Syllabus
22. Diploma in Front Office, The Complete Syllabus
23. The Time to Speak is Now
24. Munshi Premchand (Short Stories in English)
25. The Housekeeping Department, Text Book
26. Hitchhiker's Guide to Trekking in Uttarakhand
27. Uttarakhand, A divine Land for a Reason
28. Bachhon ke liye rochak kahaniyan (बच्चों के लिए रोचक कहानियाँ) (In Hindi Language)
29. Basic Communication Skills of English
30. The Basic Office Organisation Book for Start-ups
31. Hospitality HRM
32. Hospitality Marketing
33. Bakery Ingredients and Tools
34. Human Resource Management for Indian Professionals
35. The process of LAWFULLY operating a Hospitality

business in India

36. Indian Classical Sweets: History, Tradition and Recipes
37. History of India's Himalayan Cuisine: Classical Cookery of Kashmir, Laddakh, Jammu, Himachal, Lahaul, Spiti, Garhwal, Kumaon.
38. Vindu: Andhra Cuisine (Part 1 of South Indian Trilogy)
39. Saappadu: Tamil Cuisine (Part 2 of South Indian Trilogy)
40. Sadya: Malayali Cuisine (Part 3 of South Indian Trilogy)
41. South Indian Cuisine - The Researcher's Guide Book
42. The Ramayana for Children and other short stories from Indian Mythology
43. Legends of the Tribal Shiva
44. Third Generation Children's Story Book
45. It's Elementary: The Top Nine Adventures from the memoirs of Dr John H Watson (2 Editions Printed)
46. UNITY IN DIVERSITY, The foundation of Indian Tourism
47. The Thar Express: Culinary History of Rajasthan and Gujarat
48. Basics of Computerized Accounting
49. Impact (Impact of Globalization on Indian Social Life)
50. Vishnu – The Lord of Amazing Incarnations
51. Being a Mahatma in the Freedom Struggle
52. The Culinary Journey of Purvanchal: Lucknow to Patna
53. Culinary History of the Gangetic Plains
54. Indian Culinary Secrets
55. The Story of Jain and Parsi Food
56. The Great Indian Pilgrimage Tourism
57. Introduction to Tourism Studies – Text Book
58. Bread and Rolls (2 Editions Printed)
59. Diploma in Digital Marketing the Complete Syllabus
60. The Theory of Sweetened Bakery Foods
61. Campus Placement Guide for Management Trainee in

Leading Hotels

62. Diploma in Housekeeping Management, the Complete Syllabus
63. Jokes and Stories for Kids
64. Demigods of India
65. Practical Cookery Guide Book for Parents and School Teachers
66. Introduction to Cookery for Elementary School Children (Kindle)
67. The Fearless Entrepreneur (Being your own Boss)
68. Culinary Heritage of Bengal's Widow Culture
69. Journey into the Mythological Wisdom of Vedas & Puranas
70. From Stigma to Strength: The Legacy of Bengal's Widowhood
71. HAKKA: Discovering a Vibrant Community in India
72. The Indo Chinese Pot Boiler
73. Bombay Daak: *Discovering the Kolis of the Seven Islands*
74. Speak Your Mind: A Guide to Clear and Impactful Communication
75. Urbanization And Rural Dynamics In India
76. Short Stories from the Animal Kingdom
77. The Short Story Book for Children - Morals and Humour
78. Advance Tourism Studies
79. Indian Knowledge Systems
80. The Geography of India: A Comprehensive Text Book and Guide
81. The Alpha Book of Researches Volume I
82. Introduction to Management
83. Organizational Behaviour
84. Principles of Management and Organizational Behaviour
85. Advanced studies in Indian Knowledge Systems

86. MCQ Companion on Indian Knowledge Systems
87. Rivers of Justice
88. Indian Economy MCQs: 1800 Questions with answer Key for UGC NET, UPSC & Competitive Exams
89. Fundamentals of the Indian and Global Business Environment
90. Gangotri to Gangasagar: A Culinary Journey
91. Detailed History of the North Indian Cookery

Google "Dr Anshumali Pandey" for latest updates.